The Window Decorating Book

The Window Decorating Book

KATHLEEN S. STOEHR
&
CHARLES T. RANDALL

CHARLES RANDALL INC.

Published in the United States by:
Charles Randall, Inc.
Orange, California

The publisher has made every effort to ensure that all suggestions given in this book are accurate and safe, but cannot accept liability for any resulting injury, damage or loss to either person or property whether direct or consequential and however arising. With regard to the source guide you may wish to confirm colors, patterns, sizes, names or contact information. Variations in color may occur during the printing process. The publisher will be grateful for any information that will assist in keeping future editions up to date.

Copyright 2009 Charles T. Randall, www.charlesrandall.com
Printed in the United States of America
First Edition

ISBN 10: 1-890379-17-4
ISBN 13: 978-1-890379-17-9

Editor-in-Chief: Kathleen S. Stoehr
Book Interior, including photo research: Chemistry Creative
Cover Design: Beth {Burrell} Scott-Young
Cover Credits: Cover, Casa Fiora (*photo courtesy of Casa Fiora*); Back Cover, (*All*) Shutterstock. *Please refer to the Source Guide for additional information.*

Stoehr, Kathleen, 1960-
    The window decorating book / by Kathleen S. Stoehr & Charles T. Randall.
        p. cm.
    Includes bibliographical references and index.
    ISBN 1-890379-17-4
    1. Draperies. 2. Window shades. 3. Windows in interior decoration. I. Randall, Charles T. II. Title.

TT390.S87 2009
746.9'4--dc22

2009033559

CONTENTS

INTRODUCTION

ABOUT TWO MONTHS AGO, I'D HAD IT WITH MY HOME OFFICE. The walls hadn't been painted since I'd moved in 10 years prior (I know — that in and of itself is awful) and quite honestly I needed a new, fresh space.

I had the old window replaced and reframed, I painted the room a very unexpected color for my tastes — not at all the earth tones I favor, but more an odd shade of salmon. I found a patterned rug; I put a cellular shade on the window, installed cabinets. The room should have been considered done, but the window kept nagging at me. It just didn't look quite well-dressed enough. Daresay, it needed some kind of top treatment.

Being the author of a couple of books on window treatments, you might think I would have no problem selecting the treatment. But to me, my situation was more "kid in a candy store." I needed to (at least I thought I needed to) get some assistance.

Then I saw it. No — not the top treatment of my dreams…an ad in my local paper, touting "window treatment speed design." Free. One hour. Four designers. Extremely reputable design firm. Bring your window dimensions, a photo or two and any color samples you might have. I bagged an appointment for that following week.

As I sat down with each of the designers, it became clear that while each may have known a lot about what to recommend, they had no quality reference materials to show me what they had in mind. And I have to say: being a designer doesn't automatically instill great sketching skills.

It was frustrating for me to watch these four talented people flip, flip, flip through a pile of different books, trying to find just the right lambrequin or Austrian or box pleat valance to make me say, "yes!" Crazy, I know. Then they'd resort to sketching…and that didn't go over well.

Anyway…it dawned on me as I left the appointment that it was time to work on another book. One that would not just assist designers in articulating what they wanted to sell, but also to help consumers decide what they wanted on their windows. Instead of setting up window treatments by color or room or period, I decided to put together a compendium of sorts. And here it is.

Of course, because I began working on this book, I still look up at my office window and sigh. Yep — it hasn't been finished yet. The cellulars are lovely in their pinky-salmon tone but…Hmmm…top treatments begin on page 192. Now that I'm done, maybe I should start there.

Thanks so much for picking up this book. As always, I appreciate your support in bringing beautiful window treatments to every home, everywhere.

Kathleen S. Spoehr

What Works Best
A Treatment for Every Window

WHAT WORKS BEST? Here are some recommendations:

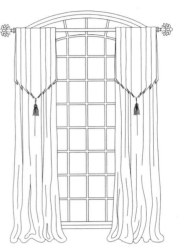

Arch (Palladian): Horizontal blinds; pleated & cellular shades; shutters; top treatments (such as cornices or scarves); some fabric treatments; some alternatives

Bow and Bay windows: Same as above

Corner window: Blinds; curtains & draperies; shades; shutters (stationary only); top treatments (all kinds); alternatives

Double hung: Blinds (horizontal, vertical); curtains & draperies; shades (pleated, cellular, Roman, roller); shutters; top treatments (all kinds); alternatives

Fixed pane: Blinds (horizontal, vertical); curtains & draperies; shades (pleated, cellular, Roman, roller); shutters; top treatments (all kinds); alternatives

French doors: Blinds; some fabric treatments such as hourglass; all types of shades; some small top treatments, such as cornices; shutters

In-Swinging Casement: Blinds; pleated & cellular shades; shutters

Picture windows: All categories

Ranch (strip) windows: Blinds; some fabric treatments; all categories of shades

Skylights: Horizontal blinds; pleated & cellular shades

Sliding glass doors: Vertical blinds; pleated & cellular shades; shutters

This fabulous flip topper drapery panel is a bold statement in the dining room area, with its luscious bullion fringe grazing the floor and eye catching contrast lining accenting with complementary tassel. A visual and tactual delight, this panel treatment enhances the area without blocking the doorframe. Design by Sharon Binkerd, Interiors by Decorating Den

Above illustration: Flip topper panels over wood rod. Custom rendering by DreamDraper® design software, www.dreamdraper.com © 2009 Evan Marsh Designs, Inc.

Question Yourself

WHILE A BASIC WINDOW TREATMENT WILL COVER YOUR BARE WINDOW, it will not necessarily address other requirements you may have. Window treatments are not just about beauty but also privacy, sun protection, sound absorption and more. Take some time to ponder the points listed below. When you sit down with a window treatment professional, he or she will ask your opinion on these topics. The better prepared you are to thoughtfully answer them the more satisfied you will be with the end result.

Existing Treatments
- What don't you like about your existing window coverings?
- Quick — what's your dream window covering? Did any thought immediately pop into your head? Write it down and save it for later reference.
- Where is your window located?
- What is currently on the window? Do you think it could be removed easily? Do you wish to retain it in some capacity?
- What are the approximate measurements of your window?
- Is the window non-traditional in shape (bay, bow, transom, etc.) or do you have mismatched windows in the same room?

General Questions
- Have you given any thought to your budget? Do a little research online and also check "The Facts" boxes located in each chapter. Costs for treatments can vary considerably.
- Is this a window that will be used frequently, as in, will you be operating the treatment and/or the window daily, weekly, monthly?
- Consider sound. If the room is noisy, would you like fabric at the window to help absorb the sound?
- Who lives in your home? Children, pets, adults, elderly? How might your window treatment affect those who dwell in your home?
- Are you interested in motorizing your window treatments? Consider motorization for any application, but particularly for hard to reach areas or treatments you may have difficulty operating. See page 13 for further details.
- Would you consider employing the services of an interior or window treatment designer?

Qualities Needed
- How long do you expect to keep this treatment?
- Does it need to be moisture resistant?
- What types of safety issues might you have? (i.e., are small children or pets in your home)
- Are you interested in championing "Green" design? (As in, do you want to select a window covering fabricated with environmentally responsible practices employed?)
- How important is energy conservation?

Time Frame/Installation

- How quickly do you hope to have your window treatment installed?
- Is this something you want to install on your own or do you plan to hire someone?
- Do you feel confident that you can measure your window precisely?

Design Thoughts

- If your room is already decorated to your satisfaction, how will this new window covering fit into that scheme?
- If you are completely redesigning your room, what is your design style? Do you prefer a soft, romantic look or a warm, traditional appearance? (Don't worry if you don't know — as you page through this book, you may discover a style that's just right for you.)
- Is this window something you wish to emphasize — or de-emphasize?
- Do you want to be able to maintain some kind of view (i.e., ensure privacy but still be able to enjoy sunlight)?
- Are there any architectural hindrances, such as window cranks, radiators, unsightly moldings, light switches, etc.?
- Is your room shaped oddly, such as a low ceiling, or is it narrow?

Finishes, Colors & Patterns

- Consider texture. How does a heavy velvet drapery compare to a sleek horizontal blind, to a lacy roller shade? Different textures make different statements.
- Pattern can add interest and depth to a plainly designed room or make it appear smaller and wider. How do you feel about decorative fabric patterns? Stripes? Checks? Florals? Small details?
- Color can tie together disparate elements in the room through a unifying tone, make a bold statement or soften harsh lines. What kinds of colors do you like best? How will they fulfill the needs of your design scheme?

Maintenance/Protection

- What type of stain, soil and/or odor protection are you concerned about?
- Do you have animals that may claw a treatment out of the way to look outside?
- Will fabric at the window be affected by direct sunlight?
- Do you smoke or have a wood burning fireplace?

Feeling good about utilizing the design services of a professional begins with your own involvement. This sitting area offers a variety of patterns pulled together to a cohesive whole through the use of red and gold tones.

Design by Ontario Design Group, Interiors by Decorating Den

Hiring an I.D.

Get over your fears.

IT IS A COMMON FEAR. Hiring an interior designer effectively releases the design of your space into a stranger's hands. You no longer have control. He or she will enter your residence like a crazed diva, throwing hands up in the air, tsk-tsking about your current look and then submitting bills that would gag a gazillionaire. First, you definitely don't want to live through the embarrassment of showing off your current interior to a professional and second — what if you pay a lot of money for something you don't even like but were too intimidated to say so?

It's time to get over your fears and accept that you not only need a designer's opinion; you will probably save money, too. They won't be like you, pacing around the local fabric store, trying to decide if it's buttercup or lemon yellow chintz you want. They aren't going to buy 10 yards at $49.99 a yard, coerce your mother to sew panels, then hang them up too low and cry when they look ghastly and overpowering.

They won't measure three times for 12 windows worth of blinds, place the order, then when it comes to installation — discover the measurements were still done improperly.

So, how do you reconcile yourself with hiring an interior designer and feel good about the process? It's called teamwork. Designers aren't mind readers — they need your help. Here's how you can make it easier on yourself and get what you want.

it is time to accept that you need — and will come to value — the opinion of a qualified professional

- Pick up a few design magazines. Clip out the rooms that appeal to you. Soon you will find there is a common thread running through the photos you have selected. Perhaps you find that all the rooms have a blue/green coloration. Maybe you're discovering that the photos you pull are all of minimally decorated rooms. Now, put these photos into a file you can produce when your designer asks you, "What are you thinking about for this room?"
- Interview prospective designers and review their portfolios. You will find that some designers specialize in a particular era of design that is not of your interest; another may just not be a good personality match; while another may be exactly what you were hoping for.
- Discuss your lifestyle and don't hold back. If you have pets, children, if you smoke — all this will be taken into consideration. Be sure, too, to complete the "Question Yourself" area on page 8–9 of this book, and share it with your designer.
- Talk about fees up front. Despite that this project is personal, you are conducting business. There is a variety of ways designers charge: some by the hour, some by a percentage of the project fee, some with a flat fee for the entire job. Then, get it in writing. Sign a contract that clarifies everything, from time frame to cost overruns to the designer's regular appearance on the job site to how often you would like them to update you on progress. When you are in agreement, emotions can remain professional and both sides feel protected.
- Finally, talk about your needs. Don't say 'yes' to something unless you are certain it is what you want. Most designers will respect that greatly. Despite that this is a creative profession, a designer is in business to serve your needs, not their own. Your happiness is their triumph.

When you must reach over a piece of furniture to operate your window treatment, consider the ease of motorization to make your life a little easier. These wood blinds are an elegant accent in an eclectic office area with their neat appearance, yet the casegood and tall plant make their daily operation somewhat difficult. A battery operated or low voltage motorization system would solve this problem simply.

The Window Decorating Book

Motorization

Battery operated or hard wired? How to decide.

ONE ITEM THAT WILL NOT BE DIRECTLY ADDRESSED in this book, except for this page, is the topic of motorization. It is a common occurrence to be able to push a button and change a television channel or open a garage door remotely. But have you considered the possibilities of motorizing your window treatments? There are several kinds of motorization, but which type is best for you depends almost entirely on the window treatment(s) you are interested in motorizing, and your budget. In general terms, however, you can look to three types of possible applications: battery operated, low voltage and hard wired.

Battery Operated

Inexpensive to install, battery-operated motorization systems also require more regular maintenance than the other two types. This is mostly due to the fact that batteries need to be changed occasionally. Consider, too, that in areas where you may need to use a motor control most (such as a skylight system) you will need a pretty high ladder to change that battery! Also, if you are planning to motorize more than one treatment within a room, it is safe to say that battery-operated systems are not entirely practical, because they do not offer "group" control options. However, if you have an easy-to-access, lightweight treatment (such as a pleated shade) that you want to be able to operate with the push of a button, the battery system is a good, easy, affordable choice.

consider that you can also ensure your privacy with motorization: no more standing in a dark window at night closing your blinds, while the lights blaze in your livingroom

Low Voltage

This type of system, easier to install than a hard-wired system, is a plug in style that can easily operate a group of window treatments with the push of a button. Ideal for "smaller" treatments (such as a group of blinds or shades), it is smaller and quieter than a hard-wired system. The downside to this type of electrical product is that it is reliant upon its voltage and that longer wire lengths or varied rotation speeds don't always deliver with the most efficiency.

Hard Wired

With the greatest capacity for lifting, drawing and tilting, a hard wired treatment is the most hardworking of the motorized systems. This is the sytem you will need, for example, to draw heavily lined and interlined velvet draperies; the kind of draperies no human could comfortably move day in and day out. But hard wired motors make it easy to accomplish. The downside to hard wiring is that it is best mapped out and installed in pre-construction, rather than afterward — though it can be done either way.

Home automation is not a new concept, but the industry is fast growing and ever changing, offering new possibilities and levels of convenience. From shades that will lower at the first hint of a darkening sky to those that are synchronized to open and close while you are away on vacation, to the ease of covering a skylight with the touch of a button, motorization makes life a little simpler. Ask your designer about the possibilities for your home.

Designing on a photo provides the most realistic portrayal of a proposed treatment, complete with any color or fabric pattern. Skewing capabilities permit the treatment to be constructed from any angle.

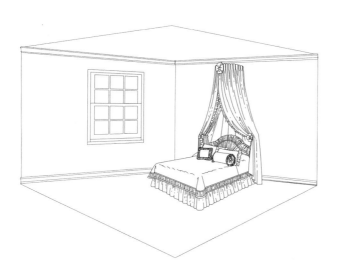

The design and graphics capabilities of the DreamDraper® software enable you to create colorful perspective renderings of a total room setting, including window treatments, bedding and furniture.

Alternative room arrangements, window treatments, furniture, wall colors and flooring are easily shown. Furniture and accessories imported from vendor websites complete the picture.

The Window Decorating Book

Software

The key to helping you visualize your dreams.

COMPUTER RENDERING OF WINDOW TREATMENT STYLES IS RAPIDLY BECOMING THE NORM in interior design. Pioneered by the DreamDraper® design program (www.dreamdraper.com), this approach allows you to take an uploaded photo or architectural rendering and effectively use that image as a canvas to further showcase a variety of window treatment styles, as well as different fabrics, patterns and colors.

It's not magic, but it may certainly seem that way. This visual communication tool will help prevent costly mistakes and take the guesswork and uncertainty out of what may otherwise be an agonizing choice over what is most appropriate for a particular window.

The DreamDraper® program offers the opportunity to personalize any window with beautiful treatments, embellishments, specialty hardware — and even layer the computer-designed treatment behind existing furniture in your photo so you can see exactly how the treatment will appear when you walk into your room. Add in wall color or paper if you like, too! No more using a paper grid and counting boxes, this program can do it all to scale.

An extensive library of beautifully illustrated window treatment styles from swags to goblet pleats to blinds to shades, decorative hardware, embellishments, and even furniture and accessories is available for you or the interior design professional. Detailed drawings are available in many different design styles, be it modern, traditional, contemporary, Art Deco and more.

it's not magic, but it may certainly seem that way. Visual communications software will prevent costly mistakes.

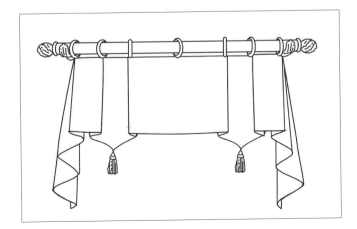
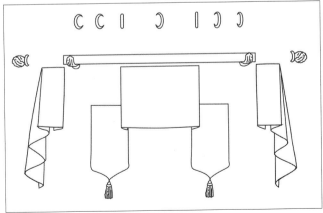

Break-apart® designs and thousands of design elements available within the DreamDraper program allow for unlimited creativity. All can be resized, modified, mixed and matched, and shown in any color or fabric.

Shutters

The clean lines and perfect function of a shutter are a true joy to behold, enhancing any interior with beautiful permanence. Louvers operate smoothly to vary light penetration from full on bright to complete darkness; offer a warm, traditional appearance; and insulate effectively

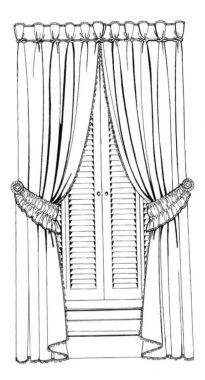

from cold and heat. The most beautiful of wood shutters are constructed with the same attention to detail and loving care as fine furniture. The most ingenious of environmentally friendly faux shutters can withstand the dampest of environments. It seems there's nothing that shutters *can't* do.

Left: French door cutouts within this shutter help control interference with the lever handles. Note that the shutter should be measured to fit outside the span of the window glass so as to allow proper installation, which may then require extension blocks or spacers to allow clearance.

Above: Goblet pleated panels with ruffled tiebacks over shutters.

History in the Making

During the era of Europe's Tudor and Elizabethan periods, wood shutters were the primary window covering. Installed on the inside of the home, these shutters were all about function. When closed, they were capable of covering the entire window to protect from rain, sunlight and intruders, oftentimes standing in for glass, due to its great expense. When open, they folded against the inner walls to act as decorative panels.

As architecture changed and windows became increasingly recessed, shutters moved outdoors to endow decoration to the exterior. Painted shutters on North American and European homes provided a pop of delicious color. Late nineteenth century improvements, such as the capability to manipulate louvers, presented a homeowner with additional options. Two tier panels (also known as Dutch shutters), offering the choice of opening just part of the shutter or all of it, and hinges to provide vertical swing, brought shutters back into the interior.

Left: Dramatic window accents can be beautiful, but if too much light enters a room, furnishings can take a beating. Consider covering your window with a specialty shaped shutter, which will cut down on glare yet still offer a winning look.

Above: Shutters can accommodate unique shapes.

Today's Shutters

Today, shutters can be found both indoors and out, offering more than just protection from the elements: exceptional beauty, terrific insulation, a variety of light control options and a life expectancy unmatched by most other window coverings. Plus, you can consider shutters an investment—most are appraised into the value of a home.

And, the industry is growing at a rapid pace. As reported in *Draperies & Window Coverings*, a magazine for window treatment trade professionals, shutters are a billion dollar industry. Representing approximately 14 percent of the total window coverings market, shutters are showing signs of continued growth and consumer interest. There is significant expansion in the affluent middle-class market population; homeowners are upgrading to these quality, high-end products without question.

Combine shutters with fabric to soften their hard lines or leave them beautifully, distinctively elegant. Comb through the variety of options: plantation, roller, accordion, arch top, Bermuda and more. With louvers from as little as ¾" to as wide as 5½" inches to suit your needs, there's a shutter waiting for you.

Art glass inserts in these solid wood shutter panels let natural light in from the outside, while louvers situated below the glass continue to provide privacy.

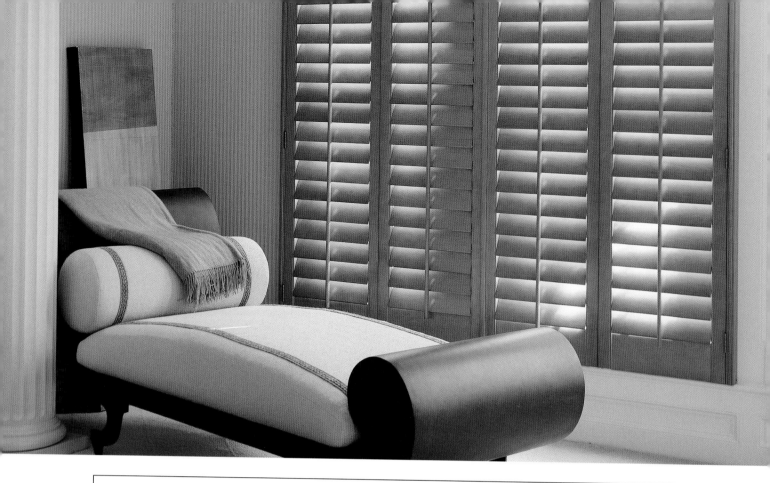

The Facts: Wood Shutters

Advantages: Natural and warm; insulates well; bridges the gap between design styles; high structural integrity; recyclable; can be painted or stained to match any décor; self-squaring frames have eliminated much of the difficulty of installation; prices have dropped due to the product becoming more accessible and available; specialty sizes offer plenty of options

Disadvantages: Not as effective in areas where water, humidity and/or moisture may be a problem, such as bathrooms; wood can warp, crack or split due to fluctuations in humidity; louvers can accumulate dust quickly if not manipulated/cleaned often; rigid; occasional unpredictable louver quality, especially with painted surfaces; lead time to acquire product can sometimes be lengthy, depending upon manufacturer

Cost: Costs will vary depending upon the type of shutter style selected (see "Good to Know" for descriptions), the size of the shutter needed, configurations, and finally, whether it is stained, unstained or painted. They can also be priced by the square foot or by square inch. However, a "normal" double hung window approximately 30" wide by about 42" high will equate to a shutter somewhere in the area of about $200–$400.

Lifespan: Decades

Most Appropriate Locations: Kitchens, living and dining rooms, bedrooms, dens, offices. Do not install in areas of high moisture, such as a bathroom. Interior and exterior applications, although exterior requires regular maintenance.

Care & Cleaning: Minimum maintenance. Use a feather duster or soft cloth to remove dust accumulation between the louvers—be sure to manipulate the louvers tilted up, then down, to remove all accumulation; washing is not recommended as, despite being sealed, the wood can discolor or warp; vacuuming with brush attachment is also effective.

Left: Three and a half inch louver wood shutters in maple are a sleek accent in a room devoted to relaxation.

Above: In a sunny window seat area, too much sun will ruin fabrics and heat up the room. Classic shutters keep it bright and fit perfectly into the bay window. Tilt bars let the user to control the degree of privacy.

Below: Pristine bi-fold shutters offer yet another way to let the sunshine in. Remember that there will be some amount of stackback, so furniture needs to be clear of those affected areas.

The Facts: Faux Wood & Vinyl Shutters

Advantages: Moisture and fire resistant, these shutters can be used in areas of high moisture; will not warp, crack or split due to environmental introductions such as moisture; can insulate better than wood; environmentally friendly; bridges the gap between design styles; recyclable; vinyl-clad wood shutters have solved the paint/durability problem

Disadvantages: Louvers can accumulate dust quickly if not manipulated/cleaned often; rigid; a cheaper brand may not duplicate the look of a wood product as much as you desire; typically not as flexible when it comes to matching more unusual color tones

Cost: Costs will vary depending upon the type of shutter style selected (see "Good to Know" for descriptions), the size of the shutter needed, configurations and finishes. Typically, however, a "normal" double hung window approximately 30" wide by about 42" high will equate to a shutter somewhere in the area of $150–$300.

Lifespan: Decades

Most Appropriate Locations: Kitchens, bathrooms, living and dining rooms, bedrooms, dens, offices. Interior and exterior applications.

Care & Cleaning: Minimum maintenance. Use a feather duster or soft cloth to remove dust accumulation between the louvers — be sure to manipulate the louvers tilted up, then down, to remove all accumulation; for more difficult soils, use a soft cloth and a mild detergent/water solution; vacuuming with brush attachment is also effective.

Left: Behind this bed stands a large window wall, an area difficult to treat for many reasons, among them privacy, insulation from cold and heat and also light control. Installing shutters creates a sense of great privacy, due to their permanent, sturdy nature, but also allows louvers to be controlled to let sun in when required. Stationary draperies flanking the bed soften this area and tie together the design motif throughout the room. Plus, it was wise to choose white shutters, rather than wood tone, in order to blend with the environment rather than become a focal point.

Above: Shutters are also available in a synthetic fabrication, striking a balance between the need for durability and the look of real wood. They are perfect for rooms with high humidity such as this bathroom area, and are as beautiful as they are practical and affordable.

Shutters

Previous page:
Above: Shabby chic shutters offer an enchanting change of style.

Below left: Capturing the natural beauty of real wood, these shutters are constructed from premium hardwood and feature the centuries-old craft tradition of fine dovetail joinery combined with an innovative multiple-coat finish.

Below right: An inviting, old world feel.

This page, above: Bi-fold shutters are a great way to cover larger windows, and typically are installed on a track to steady the panels when they are operated. Remember, also, when choosing solid wood shutters, that the beauty and natural variations of wood may show through a colored stain, no matter how dark.

This page, right: Stationary pinch pleat draperies soften four-paneled shutters.

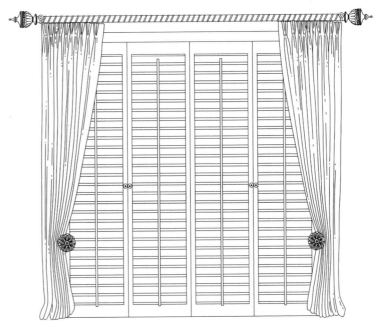

Good to Know: Wood Versus Faux

There are a variety of shutter products on the market today. Here's a look.

Metal: Typically used as an exterior product in areas of high hurricane probability, steel shutters are preferred over aluminum for better strength and protection. Large and heavy, care should be used when installing due to potentially sharp edging. Typically, these "hurricane" style shutters are removable in the non-tumultuous "off" seasons and pack together well for storage.

Polycore: An aluminum core is inserted into the center of solid polymer as it is being extruded. A synthetic material that mimics the look of wood, this material will not chip, fade or warp over time and can be cleaned with a typical citrus-style product. The aluminum reinforcement allows shutters to be constructed in lengths up to 36" wide, maximizing light control. Its capacity to withstand the hazards of moisture make this a product capable of being used anywhere in the home.

Polywood™: A synthetic wood substitute, this material is made from natural gas products and is water and fire resistant. It also withstands peeling, chipping, staining, cracking, bowing and warping. Easy to clean and care for, Polywood products will work in any area of the home, but particularly in areas of high moisture, such as a bathroom. Environmentally friendly, this product typically comes with a lifetime guarantee.

Thermalite™: A solid, non-toxic, synthetic material, Thermalite is a dense, polymer foam product that greatly resembles wood. Water resistant, fire retardant, and stated to be more than two times greater at insulating than wood, no natural resources are destroyed in its manufacturing process.

Vinyl: Even the most expensive of vinyl shutters will still result in a product less costly than wood or metal. This is a good thing for those on a budget who can't resist the allure of this solid product. Dents and scratches will not show as readily, as the color of the louver extends throughout the product. This product works well in wet environments. Limitations include the capability to choose from a wide color range and also, vinyl does not look like wood. There is the possibility for warpage, which is lessened with the addition of metal reinforcement in the louvers.

Wood: Attractive and strong, this natural product offers both beauty and strength. Its wood grain is unmatched in appearance; no two pieces of wood could ever be absolutely alike, so if you are looking for one-of-a-kind, natural beauty, wood is your option. Superior construction techniques allow wood panels to accommodate areas much longer and wider than ever. However, if your area is prone to moisture or if you prefer to clean with a water/chemical solution, wood may not be your best choice. As always, wood is recyclable. Typically made from poplar (least expensive), basswood (moderate) or alder (most expensive).

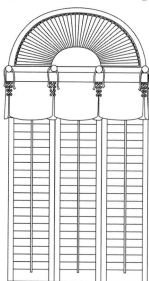

(Left) Three panel shutters under valance with treated arch. DreamDraper® design software, www.dreamdraper.com © 2009 Evan Marsh Designs, Inc.

The right shutter can instantly transform a room into an elegant, feminine retreat. And consider the difficulty of molding fine hardwood into specialty shapes, such as the arches (right). The purchase of a shutter is considered an upgrade for the home and is frequently added into the value of a property.

Good to Know: Types of Shutters

Improperly installed shutters are far too frequent a mistake. Above all else, when installing shutters, make sure the louvers angle up when the shutter is open. This is because (most especially when installed outside), driving rain will slough away and down toward the ground rather than into an upward reaching louver — and then into your home.

Also remember that there are truly no standard window sizes. Each shutter should be made to custom fit your window. Here are some of the most popular styles:

Accordion: A shutter with a unique, vertical, folding blade system. Designed to cover a large expanse of glass quickly.

Bahamas (Bermuda): An exterior shutter, it can be crafted from metal, wood or vinyl. While beautiful, its primary function is security and protection from severe storms. The difference is that this shutter is hinged at the top and opens out from the window like an awning.

Café: A smaller-style shutter used to cover only the bottom half of a window, for a combination of privacy and sunshine.

Eyebrow: A sunburst shutter (*see definition on next page*), but it is wider than it is high.

Panel: A shutter panel on a track system, or a folding shutter, often used to cover a sliding glass door. Can sometimes have fabric, woven wood or glass inserts.

Plantation: The name evoking mansions of the South, Plantation shutters have louvers over two inches wide and can even be over four inches wide. Panels are typically installed into the casement of a window.

Roller: Typically installed over a window, it can fit into that area in a number of ways, including to the wall surrounding the window, into the eave above a window or in the window reveal. For security and

Above: Shutters with tie top valance. DreamDraper® design software, www.dreamdraper.com © 2009 Evan Marsh Designs, Inc.

Left: A combination of louvers and natural woven panel insets are unique and lovely. Choose large louvers, such as the 2½" shown here, for best outside viewing.

Combined with the wood wall paneling, these shutters become part of the value of the home. Gorgeous and uniquely natural, this room absolutely glows with power and beauty, a stunning combination.

protection from storms, this shutter operates on a mechanism that rolls it into place. Can be operated from inside a building.

Shutter blinds: Combines the larger louvers of the shutter with the ease of blind operation. Resemble wood blinds.

Storm/Hurricane: For southern U.S. properties and homes extending into the Caribbean, storm shutters are crucial to secure and protect dwellings during inclement weather. Although recent climate events have shown us that sometimes we are powerless to protect our homes from the magnitude of a violent storm, storm shutters go a long way to deflect torrential wind and water. While the home may stand after a hurricane, a poorly protected window may allow too much water to enter. Note that most highly protective shutter systems need time to be fitted and installed effectively. This is the type of window covering that requires planning and a reasonable timeframe for installation. Storm shutters are available in many kinds of materials, although metal is recommended for dire weather conditions.

Sunburst: Constructed in the shape of an arch, the sunburst pattern is so named due to its design in the form of "rays," all emanating from a central point usually on the bottom edge of the piece.

Specialty sizes are considered an important and necessary part of growing a shutter business. Quarter circle, half circles, tunnels, octagons, ovals, hexagons and more are available and waiting for your important window.

Left: Eyebrow and single panel shutters enhance the architecture beautifully with traversing drapery panels to soften the area.

Right: Two and one half inch louver wood shutters finished in a soft white brighten this earth tone interior and help to enhance the earthy southwestern design style.

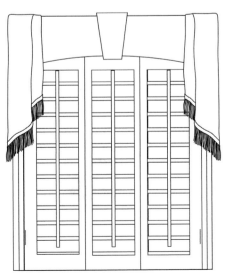
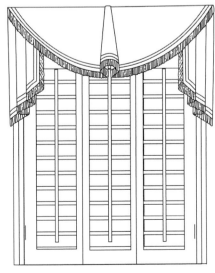

Right: Three paneled shutters with soft valances.
DreamDraper® design software, www.dreamdraper.com © 2009 Evan Marsh Designs, Inc.

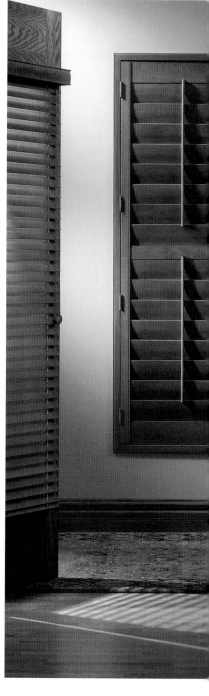

Left: It would be a shame to cover the beautiful arch extending above the French doors. This designer wisely chose to leave the arch untreated and then extended the easy and undemanding neutral tones throughout the room, making the viewing area above the fireplace a focal point. Soothing and calm, this room exudes relaxation. Shutters on the French doors are a perfect choice.

Middle: Notice how the four shutter panels offer individual control but can also swing open to allow full sun to enter the room. One caveat: the accent table to the right of the shutter would need to be moved out of the way so as not to be bumped. Furniture arrangement is something that needs to be considered when a window treatment doesn't neatly fold up into a headrail.

Right: In a room where the focal point is very clearly the gorgeous rug, it is wise to not split the focus and make the windows compete for attention. That's why the three panel shutter system is such an excellent choice. Offering complete privacy and sun control when closed with the simple tilt of a bar, the eye is allowed to travel around the room and rest at the floor. A very successful design strategy.

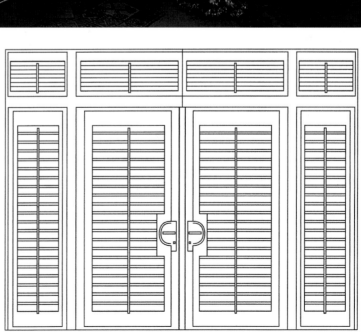

Above: A large bank of shutters over French door and adjoining windows. Custom rendering by DreamDraper® design software, www.dreamdraper.com © 2009 Evan Marsh Designs, Inc.

The Window Decorating Book

Above left: These specialty shaped shutters showcase the latest advances in wood composite technology and offer two distinct louver configurations: a movable louver and the stationary, horizontal louver (*shown*). Composite shutters are a perfect choice for areas of high moisture or potential for warpage, but are also beautiful in any area of the home. Surface integrity, durability and color consistency are just some of the highlights of composite systems.

Below left: Bright white wood shutters bring energy and appeal to a child's bedroom and can easily transition to adulthood with this or subsequent occupants.

Below right: Shutters can add style and flair to intimate spaces such as bedrooms and the advanced composite materials help maintain their elegant appearance for years.

This page, below: Three and one half inch louvers offer the best kind of viewing possibilities when open, and full privacy and sun coverage when closed.

This page, right: Austrian shade over full shutters. Custom rendering by DreamDraper® design software, www.dreamdraper.com © 2009 Evan Marsh Designs, Inc.

Above: Classic stained wood shutters with 3½" louvers impart a built-in look that will last for decades.

Left: Hardwood shutters add timeless appeal to this den, capturing the beauty of wood effortlessly.

Consider how in both of these applications, the shutters have become part of the room's architectural appeal. This is truly the only category of window treatment that can boast such an amazing capability.

Below: Hardwood shutters mix with glass panes.

Good to Know: Shutter Components

Shutters are typically comprised of the following pieces:

1. **Rails (including top, divider and bottom):** These pieces are structural and range in height from approximately two inches to about 4½" high depending upon the height of the panel and size of the louver.
2. **Louvers:** Rotating on a pin and connected together by a tilt bar, these individual pieces can vary in size from a typical standard 1¼" up to over four inches, depending upon the material used and type of shutter product.
3. **Tilt Bar:** Connected to each of the individual louvers in the center, the tilt bar controls the light, privacy and ventilation associated with the shutter. Usually moves only up and down.
4. **Stiles:** The right and left structural pieces, which aid in holding the shutter together. Usually about two inches wide and holds the pins in place that connect to the louver.

The value of shutters lies in their extreme durability and classic beauty. Fabric treatments, as well as most shades and blinds, will succumb to normal wear and tear. Shutters are capable of remaining in their original high quality state for decades, if not centuries. Light and privacy control can vary from fully opening them away from the window for a full view, to closing the louvers for an almost black-out effect.

Left: Simple shutters, softened with floral ring top drapery panels, are bright and easy to operate.
Design by Virginia Smith, ASID, DDCD, Interiors by Decorating Den; photo by Ken Vaughan

Middle: Large shutters in French door style will swing out to allow access to the glass. Design by
Pa,ela Sarmiento, Interiors by Decorating Den; photo by Zack Benson

Right: With a subtle arch top, shutters mirror the architecture and also are perfect in areas where
other window treatments might impede the ability to sit and enjoy the window seat. Design by
Angela Palmer, Interiors by Decorating Den; photo by Jeff Sanders

Previous page

Above left: Beautiful wood shutters with large slats go hand-in-hand with the elaboate woodwork. Design by Angela Palmer, Interiors by Decorating Den; photo by Jeff Sanders

Below left: Shutters can be painted to any color. Design by Sarah Barnard, Sarah Barnard Design

Below right: Simple shutters in a child's room are a good standard treatment to last years and years. Design by Sarah Barnard, Sarah Barnard Design

This page (below): Notice how the larger slats on the shutters allow better viewing of the outdoors. Design by Susan Owens, Interiors by Decorating Den; photo by Richard Ruthkatz

This page (right): Puddled, blouson tab tops over three panel shutters. Custom rendering by DreamDraper® design software, www.dreamdraper.com © 2009 Evan Marsh Designs, Inc.

When there isn't a lot of room for a window treatment, shutters can fill the bill well. Design by Sandra Valdes Interiors by Decorating Den; photo by Jeff Snyder.

Shutters are perfect for a dining room when furniture may obstruct the outward movement.

Softened with stationary fabric panels, these shutters are all about privacy.
Design by Nancy Barrett, Interiors by Decorating Den

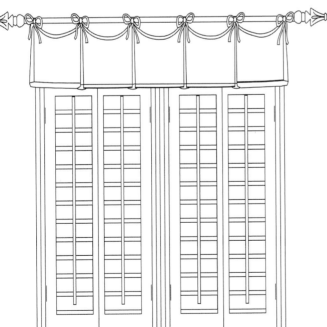

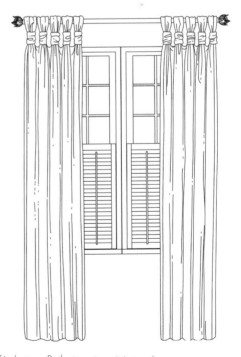

Above: Tie top valance over café shutters; Designer tab top drapery panels over café shutters. Both: DreamDraper® design software, www.dreamdraper.com © 2009 Evan Marsh Designs, Inc.

(*Left*) Water resistant shutters are a great choice for spa-style bathrooms.

(*Right*) A perfect choice for behind a tight area, these shutters can swing open, or just rotate up or down.

(*Left*) Plantation-style shutters enhance the decor and are softened by color-blocked drapery panels.

(*Right*) A great choice for behind a sofa, shutters are shown here in the open position, to allow maximum exposure.

Curtains & Draperies

Curtains and draperies have enjoyed their decades of excess and floundered over times of pared down minimalism. Consider all of the wonderful uses for fabric at the window: an interlined silk pinch pleat panel hanging stately in a historical home; a simple sheer brushing lazily against a window frame; a dainty gingham checked café curtain decorating a kitchen.

Fabric at the window softens edges, emphasizes (or de-emphasizes) architectural qualities and shortcomings and provides a needed barrier between the outside elements and the inner harmony of the home.

Left: Ring top panels frame the indoors (and out of doors) to perfection with fluid grace. A quick flip of the panel over the decorative holdback will allow the panels to traverse easily by hand, providing night time privacy.

Above: Puddled Athena drapery panels with bow accents.

47

History in the Making

It wasn't until the second half of the 17th century that draperies truly began to decorate homes. As you discovered in the previous chapter, shutters were the window treatment of choice for centuries. There are many reasons why fabric at the window was missing — among them, lack of industrial excellence, lack of fibers to work with (wool, silk and linen were the most easily acquired — if one considers a trip from the Far East to a French interior...via camel...*easy*), and also, simply, the trends of the time. A move to luxurious comfort did not occur until well into the 17th century, most unmistakably at French King Louis XIV's Palace of Versailles, for example.

Spinning wheels, the Industrial Revolution, increased trade routes and human ingenuity in taking the beauty of nature and color and incorporating these motifs into fabric patterns helped the drapery industry flourish. Soon, cornices, pelmets and passementerie (decorative trim) followed. Bed coverings turned lavish. Sashes pulled draperies to the side during the day, portieres (draperies for doorways) kept drafts at a minimum. Festoons (those draperies that could be pulled up on the window to create a swag effect) were followed by graceful reefed curtains. Cotton and silk fabrics replaced velvet, wool and tapestry. Layers cropped up: a window treatment of the Victorian era, for instance, might consist of four to five layers.

It is true that drapery began to occupy a pared-down role the mid to late 20th century, especially with the development of a variety of shades and blinds. While homes of the 1960s witnessed the heyday of pinch pleat draperies, the 1970s were all about horizontal and vertical blinds. Yet, the call for fabric treatments has not slowed.

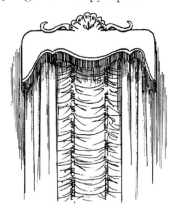

Left: Tone-on-tone white draperies and sheers are gorgeously sophisticated, coupling with lush, upholstered furniture.

Above: Cornice with stationary panels; Italian strung shade.

Today's Curtains & Draperies

Today, as windows swoop to the ceiling — and even into the ceilings of many a home — fabric at the windows is an important statement. Indeed, some designers begin with the window treatment color palette before making decisions about anything else in a room. Decisions about draperies in the home fall into distinct categories: privacy (which also includes protection); physical and visual touch; light control; sound control; and color. Put these categories in order of preference; it will make a difference. For example, if you wish for privacy at night but have your heart set on a sheer to only diffuse light during the day, you may need to add another treatment, such as a cellular shade, to take care of both needs.

Do not discount the emotion that fabric can bring to a home: the mood of an interior can be affected by the colors chosen (sunny versus somber), how light or heavy a fabric is, how casual or elegant, how romantic or businesslike. You will see examples as you page through this section. Examine the rooms. Find one similar in shape and scale to your own. Then, visualize how the treatments and fabric shown might change the look of your space.

Italian strung shades are enhanced with lush trim and also provide a beautiful backdrop to stationary side panels.

The Facts: Curtains & Draperies

Advantages: Can camouflage bad woodwork and other architectural flaws; sound absorbent; can insulate, such as masking cold air leaks in windows. Also effective in blocking the sun's damaging rays; can be a room's focal point; if lined well, can offer privacy; softens the look of hard window treatments when used in combination; mount a drapery rod at ceiling level to enhance the height of a room; colored and patterned fabric can provide visual interest.

Disadvantages: Can be affected by moisture; color can fade when exposed to direct sunlight; improper dying can cause color transfer; can harbor dust and other allergic airborne entities. In general, sun and air pollution will work against fabrics, although some are more resistant than others. Drapery linings will offer good protection and lengthen the life of your drapery.

Cost: Inexpensive drapery panels can be acquired for as little $20 at a local discount store—but if your goal is something more unique and perfectly suited for your environment, you should consider that cost may increase quite a bit. Quality, design, fiber type, linings, interlinings, embellishments and more will all factor into the price. Curtains and draperies are works of art, hand and machine sewn by talented workrooms.

Lifespan: Many variables will affect your draperies including sunlight, dust, humidity and smoke fumes to name a few. On average, however, unlined draperies will last about four years; lined about six.

Most Appropriate Locations: Bedrooms, living rooms, dens, although fabric at the window has been long accepted in any location.

Care & Cleaning: Cleaning drapery on ones own can be tricky. Vacuuming with a soft brush is acceptable. Taking a drapery down to hang on an outside clothesline is fine (as long as you know how to rehang it properly) but depending upon whether your drapery is lined and/or whether it has decorative embellishments make cleaning drapery primarily a job for experts. Consult with your local dry cleaner, or employ an onsite drapery cleaner for best results.

Left: Tab tops are a casual, yet sleek method for hanging drapery panels.

Design by Marg Anquetil, Interiors by Decorating Den

Above: Beige and green create a tranquil bedroom environment. An intricate cornice anchors this treatment, with drapery panels to balance and an operational fabric shade to provide privacy.

Design by Kris Miller, Interiors by Decorating Den

Below: Grommet topped panels are a very modern look. Note that it's possible there may be some metal upon metal noise when traversing your draperies.

Curtains & Draperies

Pretty pleated and scalloped heading ring top café curtains add softness to horizontal blinds. Lining provides extra protection from the sun.

The Window Decorating Book

Right: An upholstered cornice masks the hardware that allows the drapery to traverse. Soft and feminine, this combination is perfect for a little girls' room.

Enjoy a few more lush styles (below).
Scalloped heading with sewn-on rings, Scalloped heading with ties, Scalloped and tabbed heading; Upholstered cornice with unique detailing with double drapery panels; Checkered padded cornice over stationary drapery panels.

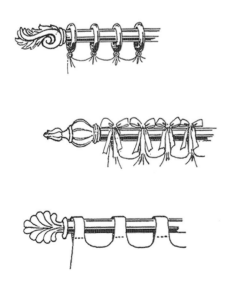

Curtains & Draperies

Good to Know: Fabrics

There are so many fabrics today. What's best for you? In general, crisp fabrics lend themselves better to tailored treatments such as café curtains and pleated draperies, while soft, pliable fabrics are terrific for puddling, swagging and draping.

Brocade: Rich and heavy, this multi-colored jacquard (*see definition*) fabric is typically used in upholstery but occasionally in draperies. Sometimes incorporates metallic threads as part of its all-over raised patterns or floral designs. Traditionally created from a background of cotton with rayon/silk patterns.

Burlap: Loosely constructed, this plain-weave jute fabric is most often seen as housing for sacks of coffee beans or as backing on some types of flooring products. However, in recent years, this rough, coarse fabric has made its way into trendy interiors, reinvented as casual draperies. Also, Jute.

Burnout: A technique used on many kinds of fabric but in general is a chemical solution applied to destroy a portion of the fabric, while leaving other areas intact. An example would be burning a floral pattern out of the pile in a velvet piece while leaving the backing fabric intact. Burnout sheers are extremely popular, as they allow light to filter through at various intensities.

Calico: Used primarily for simple curtains, this cotton fabric boasts small floral patterns (typically) on a contrasting background. An inexpensive fabric, calico is thin and not particularly colorfast, but crisp when ironed.

Canvas: A sturdy, plain weave cloth, this cotton or cotton/polyester cloth offers a stiff and tailored, yet casual look. Best for stationary drapery panels. Consider duck or sailcloth (lighter weight canvas) if you require a little bit of draping.

Chintz: This cotton cloth offers bright colors, patterns and floral motifs. Consider having this fabric lined if used in a window that receives direct sunlight, as the fabric will weaken, fade and possibly rot over time. Sometimes chintz is finished with a slight glaze to offer a polished look, although it will wash or wear off with repeated handling. Was very popular in the 18th century, though is still used frequently today due to its lower cost and bright patterns. For curtains or draperies.

Damask: A finer, thinner fabric than brocade, it nonetheless mixes shiny and dull threads to create beautiful patterns of high luster. Can be crafted of silk, cotton, rayon or linen. Its patterns are usually reversible, an example being two-color damask in which the colors reverse depending upon which side is shown. For draperies.

Dotted Swiss: A delicate lightweight cotton fabric best suited for curtains. Small raised dots printed on either side of the fabric are the identifying detail. Most often they are woven into the fabric; they can now be found applied to the surface (not as lovely).

Right: Scarf swags gracefully edge the arched window, enhancing but not hiding, it.

Short, narrow windows were corrected visually with the placement of an unusual arch top decorative rod, which adds height and drama. The blend of pink and blue can sometimes be polarizing but this combination exudes style and elegance, with the pink banding allowing the treatment to distinguish itself from similarly colored walls. Notice, too, that the vine-like scrolling on the hardware echoes the floral fabric motif.

Curtains & Draperies

Gathered stationary sheers accented with beaded tassels bring Moroccan flair to this sitting area. It is the beautiful details, such as the shaped points of the sheers, that make this treatment so successful.

Gingham: Usually seen in a plaid or checked pattern, gingham is a plain weave cotton fabric used most often for café curtains and very light draperies, such as seen in a childs' room. Typically white with one color accent.

Jacquard: Refers to a type of weave more so than a fabric. The Jacquard loom was invented in France, 1804 by Joseph Jacquard. Brocade, damask and tapestry are some of the fabrics manufactured with a jacquard attachment, which permits separate control of each of the yarns being processed.

Lace: A light, open work cotton fabric typically used for sheers or curtains, its delicate mesh background consists of openwork designs. On window treatments, it is best to choose a synthetic lace so it will hold its shape when hanging.

Linen: Stronger and glossier than cotton, linen fibers are obtained from the interior of the woody stem of the flax plant. It is strong but not pliable. It will wrinkle readily and is somewhat stiff. However, its tough, textured beauty makes it an interesting look at the window in curtain or drapery form. Excellent sun resistance.

Matelassé: Meaning "padded" or "quilted" (French), this medium to heavy double cloth fabric is usually made from silk, cotton, rayon or wool. For draperies.

Moiré: Meaning "watered" (French) this silk, rayon, cotton or acetate fabric has a distinctive wavy pattern on the surface that reflects light in the same way that light reflects off water. For draperies.

Muslin: For casual curtains and draperies, cotton muslin can be fine to coarsely woven. Typically used as liner fabric, but has been seen as the primary material. Coloration is neutral.

Nylon: Perfect for sheers, nylon is durable, washable and inexpensive.

Organza (Organdy): This lightweight, crisp, sheer cotton fabric is finished with a starch that will wash out. Will wrinkle quickly if crumpled or not finished with a wrinkle-resistant finish. Can take a variety of finishes and embellishments including bleaching, dying, frosting, flocking and more. For curtains and draperies.

Beautiful arch top draperies enhance the view without impeding egress through the French doors — a spectacular method of celebrating the architecture rather than hiding it.

Satin: With a matte back and a lustrous front, satin is available in many colors, weights and degrees of stiffness. Traditionally for evening and wedding garments, as well as high end bedding, it is sometimes used at the window. Expensive and slippery but used occasionally for drapery.

Silk: Silk is a natural filament, a product the silk worm creates when constructing its cocoon. There are many kinds of silk: tussah (a wild silk which is shorter and wider), shantung (raw and irregular) and doupioni (uneven and irregular threads) to name a few. Shiny and luxurious, it is a beautiful choice for drapery panels but will be affected by sun and water. Expensive, it is best to line and interline this fabric when used at the window, to protect it and lengthen its life.

Taffeta: A crisp fabric known best for its wonderful "rustle" sound, taffeta is a lustrous plain weave fabric usually made from synthetic fibers but sometimes made from silk. Best used for draperies, it has a crisp hand and a lot of bulk.

Tapestry: Heavy and deliciously dense, tapestry is often hand-woven and features elaborate motifs such as pictorials, floral and historical scenes. While it is never used for curtains, tapestries are frequently used as wall hangings and occasionally fitted with rod pockets to hang in front of a window. Today, tapestry is more frequently constructed on a jacquard loom.

Toile: French for fabric or cloth, toile is best known as *Toile de Jouy*, a finely printed design resembling a pen and ink drawing. Found primarily on cotton fabric, toile de jouy depicts romantic, idyllic scenes of pastoral countrysides, florals and historical motifs. For curtains and draperies.

Velvet: Plain and figured velvets are beautiful and soft, and best employed as drapery fabric. A medium weight cut-pile fabric typically constructed of silk, rayon, cotton or synthetics, its high luster and smooth hand create beautiful, graceful folds of fabric. Crease resistant and fairly inexpensive, velvet wears well and should be cut simply to accentuate its clean lines.

Voile: A lightweight, sheer fabric, cotton (also wool) voile is plain and loosely woven. Perfect for curtains or draperies, it gathers and drapes well.

Curtains vs. Draperies

These two terms are not interchangeable, at least not on American soil. Consider that curtains are a less formal choice than draperies — they are typically less heavy, lighter, shorter and more fanciful. Draperies utilize heavier fabrics, and the best of the bunch are lined to protect their beautiful colors and patterns from the sun's damaging rays. While both curtains and draperies may employ the use of passementerie (decorative trims and tassels), the trim on a curtain will typically amount to a small band of color, or a short brush fringe or perhaps a tiny row of beads, while a drapery may employ, among other things, a tassel tieback that weighs as much as a bunch of bananas.

For more information on the differences between curtains and draperies, be sure to refer to page 60 and 61.

Bolstering Your Fabric

There are many ways to keep your fabrics looking their best at the window. Always have your treatments lined, unless you specifically want light to filter through. Lining gives your drapery bulk, protection and stability — and quite honestly, most unlined drapery looks cheap. Here are options:

Interfacing: Fabrics used to offer support and give shape to the primary fabric. Some are designed to be stitched to the primary fabric; others are fused through heat.

Interlining: An insulation of sorts to pad, stiffen and protect the decorative fabric, as well as provide added insulation between the outside and the inside of the home. Interlining is sewn to the backside of the beauty fabric and then covered with the lining, which typically faces the street side of the window. Interlining is not seen but provides a great deal of protection and oomph to a drapery.

Lining: A layer attached to the backside of a decorative fabric or interlining to protect drapery fabric from sunrays and potential water damage from leaky windows. Adds bulk to a drapery.

Strong patterns create bold emphasis in these ring top draperies. Notice that the far right sofa has accent pillows in the same fabric to enhance the design impact.

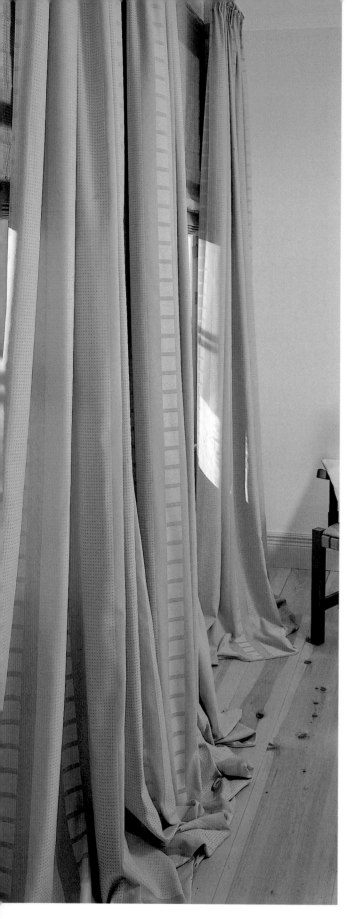

Curtain & Drapery Styles

A short tutorial

Arch-top: A treatment for the specialty shaped arch top window. A special frame is constructed with small hooks or pegs to shadow the curved area of the window. Loops are attached to this simple curved top treatment and it is hooked into place. It is a stationary treatment, although the sides can most definitely be pulled out of the way.

Bishop sleeve: Tieback draperies that have been bloused vertically at least twice and most resemble the puffy sleeve of a fancy garment.

Café curtain: Designed as a two-tier treatment, café curtains are set at a variety of heights for maximum privacy and light control, although usually at the top of a window, and then again midway. They are usually kept closed, though can traverse if necessary.

Curtain: A simple treatment, typically unlined, usually stationary or possibly hand drawn. Usually hung on a simple rod.

Drapery: A heavier treatment, lined, and able to open and close in a number of different ways. Can also be stationary, which means it flanks either side of a window, rather than hanging in front of it.

Festoon: Folded drapery fabric that hangs in a graceful curve from the top of the window, usually drawn up on cords. Also known as a swag. The term festoon can also refer to a ribbon-tied garland balanced between two points (such as either side of a window), which drapes down in the center.

Flip topper: Typically a flat, contrast lined fabric panel that flips over a rod. The flipped portion will frequently be decorated to draw attention, such as using beads or other trim and may also be cinched or triangulated in some way for added emphasis.

French pleat: A three-fold pleat found at the top of a drapery. Also known as a pinch pleat.

Goblet pleat: Similar to a pinch pleat, only the top of the pleat resembles the shape of a goblet. Sometimes the goblet is filled with batting to provide bulk, or a contrasting fabric for emphasis.

Hourglass: A permanently installed treatment that is attached at the top and bottom of a glass door or window, and then pinched in the middle to create the hourglass shape. It provides some privacy, but is mostly for decoration.

Sun-colored fabrics impart a light, upbeat mood. Ring top drapery panels, which puddle onto the floor with almost reckless abandon, are protected by complementary fabric shades. It is a tribute to the environment outside the door that bright colors are its frame.

Inverted pleat: Basically, a reverse box pleat, also known as a kick pleat, which conceals the extra fabric in back. The pleat meets in the middle, rather than is folded back at the sides.

Italian stringing: A historical way of drawing fabric in which diagonally strung cords attached to the back of the drape — about one-third of the way down — are manipulated to draw the drapery open and closed. In order for this to work, the top of the drapery must be stationary.

Knife pleat: Evenly spaced, tight, crisp, narrow pleats that run the length of the top of a drapery.

Pinch pleat: *see* French pleat

Portiere: A drapery treatment that hangs in either a doorway or room entrance. Usually stationary, its main function is to soften and beautify an area. When operational, it can serve as a sound barrier between two rooms and also alleviate drafts.

Rod pocket: A hollow tube-like sleeve located at the top of a drapery (and sometimes top/bottom of a curtain) that will accommodate a rod. The rod is attached to the wall or ceiling and the drapery, suspending from it, is able to traverse back and forth.

Sheer: A light, see-through or opaque fabric, never lined. It is only used for beauty and some sun control. Usually used in conjunction with some other hard treatment, such as cellular shades or blinds.

Stationary drape: Usually hangs to either side of the window and acts as decoration. It is not meant to provide protection from the sun or offer privacy. It is a beauty treatment that does not move.

Tab: A series of tabs at the top of the drapery, either a closed loop or a tie, which a rod either slides through, or the treatment is tied to.

Tent fold: A drapery that is constructed so as to resemble an old fashioned pup tent opening, in that the middle edge of the treatment is pulled back and secured simply, overlapping the rest of the drapery, rather than pulling it all back. Will conceal much of the window, even when open.

A curtain is a simple treatment, typically unlined and drawn by hand across a standard rod. The large scale fabric pattern is eye catching and powerful, a terrific partner to its lilting, breezy shape.

Curtain & Drapery Styles

Some of the more common curtain and drapery styles include:

This page
Upper row, top: An arch top follows the window architecture.
Upper row, middle: The bishop sleeve resembles the puffy sleeve of a fancy garment.
Upper row, right: A café curtain is a short treatment, usually spanning only half of the window.
Lower row, left: Café curtain on top of bay window only.
Lower row, middle: Cuffed curtains are slouchy and casual.
Lower row, right: Flat panel draperies are some of the easiest draperies to construct, yet look so nice!
Next page
Upper row, left: A flip top panel is a fabric panel that flips over the top of a rod.

Upper row, middle: Goblet pleats resemble a drinking goblet.
Upper row, right: Grommet top panels have generous inner rings holding the drapery in place.
Middle row, left: Pinch pleat draperies exhibit a three-fold pleat.
Middle row, middle: Ring top draperies have rings either sewn in or attached with drapery pins to allow the panel to traverse.
Middle row, right: Rod pocket treatments have a built-in pocket through which the drapery rod is fed.
Lower row, left: Tab tops take the place of rings and are similar to rod pockets, though open.
Lower row, middle: Tent fold treatments are pulled back by overlapping like a pup tent rather than in folds.
Lower row, right: Tie top treatments are attached by either knotting or bowing each individual tie to the rod.

Arch Top

Bishop Sleeve

Café Curtain

Café Curtain

Cuffed

Flat Panel

Flip Topper

Goblet Pleat

Grommet Top

Pinch Pleat

Ring Top

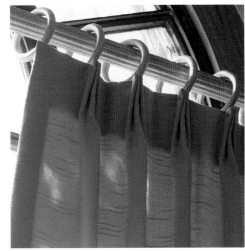

Rod Pocket

Tab Top

Tent Fold

Tie Top

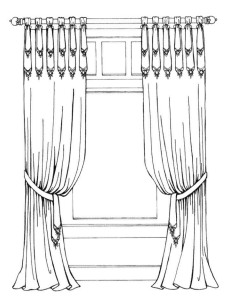

Previous page: Teal and gold ring top Parisian pleated drapery panels with ring top and black-out lining air kiss the hardwood floor — a perfect length in that the hem is much less likely to wear and also makes for easy floor maintenance. A traditional Roman shade completes this layered look.

This page:

Top left: Bold turquoise and taupe stripes pop against the large scale patterned wallcovering. This is a room with absolutely no regard for bland conventions; it is a celebration of color that succeeds completely.

Bottom left: Tab top draperies with ornamental ties.

Top right: Pinch pleat draperies cover a corner window area. This is a dramatic treatment in both color and scope.

Bottom right: Stationary panels with banded, ruffled top make an elegant statement. Custom rendering by DreamDraper® design software, www.dreamdraper.com © 2009 Evan Marsh Designs, Inc.

Top left: Simple sheers diffuse the light and allow the marble floors to glow. Pleated panels can be drawn closed if needed, with a release of the tassel tiebacks.

Bottom left: Pinch pleated draperies are color banded for added emphasis.

Top right: Full sheer treatments placed ceiling height next to a soaking tub are the epitome of luxury.

Bottom right: Puddled draperies with swag embellishment are hung slightly lower to expose decorative glass. Custom rendering by DreamDraper® design software, www.dreamdraper.com © 2009 Evan Marsh Designs

The Window Decorating Book

Ceiling height drapery treatments move on a motorized track to allow ease in opening and closing.

This soft bedroom is a cool, calm retreat with the window as its eye catching focal point. Horizontal stripes elongate the area and tie in wall and bedding tones. The short café shutters provide instant privacy; lush tassel tiebacks are easily released to envelop the room in darkness.

The Window Decorating Book

Right: This layered treatment offers capability to filter light without sacrificing full sun through the use of the sheer undertreatments. At night, cream colored draperies traverse on the rod for additional privacy.

Lower left: Goblet pleated drapery panels with flat panel Roman shade.

Lower right: Puddled blouson drapery panels, hung with rings, offer casual elegance.

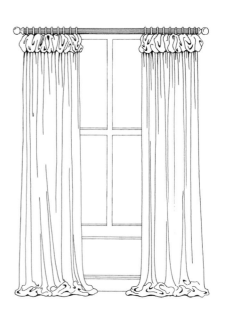

Ringtop panels hung at the same level help to even the disparate heights of the two windows and provide an inviting splash of color.

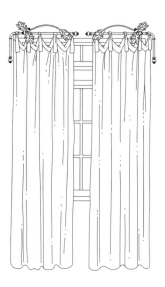
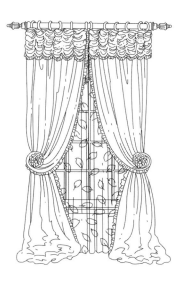

The Window Decorating Book

Chocolate brown silk panels accented with steel blue-gray floral bring warmth to the dining area and tie together all of the wood tones.

Previous page:
Left: Ring top draperies with simple braid tiebacks.
Middle: Tie top on swing arm rods.
Right: Sheer undertreatments are enhanced with puddled ring top drapery panels and gathered valance.

All illustrations: Custom rendering by DreamDraper® design software, www.dreamdraper.com © 2009 Evan Marsh Designs, Inc.

Right: Color blocked panels in the popular pink/chocolate brown tones are a winning combination in this primping area. Note how the solid tone panels help to anchor the highly decorated wallcoverings. A stylish combination.

Middle: Pretty crinkle shades are ballgown beautiful when paired with dramatic fuscia side panels dripping with beaded trim.

Left: Simple Belgian lace curtains in a 48" width unify the room, creating color harmony. The sheer fabric is a natural to maintain the dappled lightness — such an important requirement for a lazy afternoon on the sunporch.

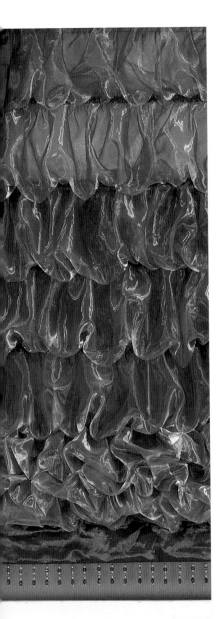

Above: Window walls receive instant privacy when covered with sheer fabric, traversing on rod pockets. The color blocked panels in water tones are an effective choice.

Left: In St. Tropez, the sun, the wind and the sea are some of life's greatest gifts. Billowing sheers set across this lookout are an indulgence, a dramatic sarong skirt, ocean colored, easy to pull aside when the sun has set.

Next page: Lush and luxuriant, rich royal blue panels hang heavy, pulled back pup tent style. This color, this style — is exceptionally rich and affluent in tone.

Above: Stationary drapery panels are capped, turban-style, with a soft contrast fabric cornice. The crisp folds of both treatments exhibit the ultimate in tailored, Old Hollywood Glamour elegance.
Design by Sheryl Tircuit McLean, Interiors by Decorating Den

Left: Traversing pinch pleated draperies placed at ceiling height help to elongate the area, making this smaller room appear larger.

Below: Bullion-trimmed swag ends in a graceful puddle. Custom rendering by DreamDraper® design software, www.dreamdraper.com © 2009 Evan Marsh Designs, Inc.

Above: With the French doors as focal points in this living area, placing the draperies at ceiling height enhances the drama. Another nice touch is the unity of the wall and drapery color. The small print on the fabric pops but doesn't overpower the walls or furnishings.

Curtains & Draperies

Above left: This ceiling height drapery treatment offers sheer drama with contrast trim pulling in tones from throughout the décor. Imagine your delight in drawing these draperies each evening, traversing neatly on the rod.

Above right: Beautifully draped panels add elegance to this bedroom. Because they are so difficult to dress, these panels should remain untouched, with the fabric shades providing nighttime privacy.

Left: A flip topper is actually a simple to construct treatment, created by flipping the top of a long drapery panel over a rod to display the contrasting lining. The cinched band makes a great focal point.

Below: Puddled flip top panels with a legacy valance. Custom rendering by DreamDraper® design software, www.dreamdraper.com © 2009 Evan Marsh Designs, Inc.

Unabashedly eye-catching, Bishop sleeves with rich coloration, coupled with overscale tassels is entirely sophisticated.

Photo courtesy of Interiors by Decorating Den

Curtains & Draperies

Above: Consider that not all draperies belong in the window area. Here, a soft cornice is mounted at ceiling height above the bed with beautiful fabric cascading behind and to the sides. This is a dramatic treatment and certainly the focal point of this room. Luscious, luscious, luscious!

Left: Rich silk panels rotate on moveable rods to allow more intimate conversation areas to be made. Lush tiebacks and sumptuous brush fringe provide eye-catching accent.

Below: Treating windows in the same room while fulfilling different needs — in this case, French doors, floor to ceiling windows and windows abutting a corner area — can be extremely difficult. In this installation, lush drapery panels enhance the room from top to bottom, creating sound buffers and visual impact, while leaving doors easy to access and tricky corners covered. Design by Lynne Lawson, Interiors by Decorating Den

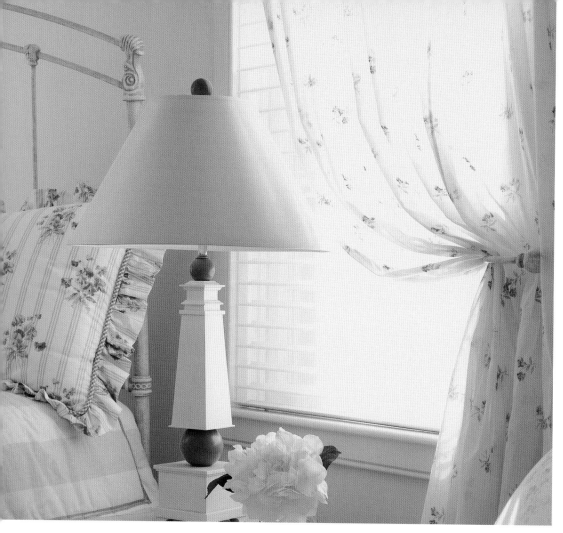

(*Left*) Pretty sheer curtains are paired flawlessly with a fabric/vane combination shade. Delightfully, unabashedly feminine!

(*Right*) This is not your typical boring laundry room! Fresh, minty tones are a perfect way to make wash day sparkle. Easy curtain panels can cover up the sunshine if necessary — but why bother? Flanking the table, they're perfect as is.

(*Left*) Delicate rod pocket curtains soften the kitchen window while offering a modicum of sun protection and clean coverage.

(*Right*) Café mount ring top panels in an icy blue are privacy lined to maintain the pretty floral fabric and keep prying eyes at bay when need be.

Above: Pole hung Empire valance enhances the stationary draperies. This symmetrical treatment becomes a sophisticated focal point in a lush master bedroom. Design by Rebecca Shearn, Interiors by Decorating Den

Left: The layered elegance of sheers coupled with lined panels is a sumptuous look. Leave just one open in the day hours; close both for evening.

Next page: The cool elegance of multiple complementary earth tones have been placed at ceiling height to add dramatic impact. Removable tiebacks allow drapes to fall easily into privacy mode and despite their sophisticated styling, these draperies are a cinch to pull back into submission, come daylight.

Above left: Stationary flip top drapery panels set into this bay window are a chic focal point coupled with fabric/vane combination shades. Design by Barbara Elliot & Jennifer Ward Woods, Interiors by Decorating Den

Middle Left: Dramatic earth tone plaid draperies sweep from floor to ceiling. This is a bold design choice that pays off bigtime. Design by Allison Havill Todd, Interiors by Decorating Den

Lower Left: Stylishly pleated drapery panels are a soothing accent in this natural dining area.

Below: A portiere is a drapery-style treatment used in a doorway instead of the usual window. Perfect in rooms where additional sound buffering is needed (such as a dining area), the portiere frames a doorway in soft elegance—or in some cases, even serves as a door. Design by Sharon Binkerd, Interiors by Decorating Den

The focal point is fabric. Cleverly styled, this treatment is known as a tent flap, displaying its contrast fabric when held up and out of the way. Privacy is provided by the matching shades.

Luxurious gold drapery panels are edged in passementerie, and layered over a lighter sheer treatment.

An unusual color but bound to be eye-catching, orange sheers capture attention in a most delicate manner.

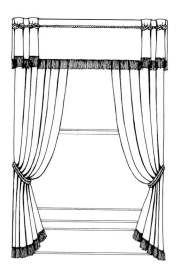

Left: Soft cartridge pleated cornice trimmed in brush fringe with pleated drapery panels.

Right: Sheer drapery treatments soften the view without masking it entirely. An asymmetrical pole swag tops this treatment in style.

Green sheers offer a pop of color and yet offer a veiled view of outside.

Pleated draperies and a cellular shade combine for a rich, compelling treatment.

Design by Patty Hughes, Interiors by Decorating Den; photo by Dennis Stierer

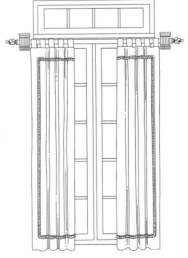

Left: A two-layered treatment incorporates a sheer side panel, held back with tassel tieback and asymmetrical pole swag with bullion fringe and tassel tieback.

Right: Tab top panels glide easily on decorative rod. Custom rendering by DreamDraper® design software, www.dreamdraper.com © 2009 Evan Marsh Designs, Inc.

Above: Big goblet pleats are a lovely accent, drawing the eye upward. Sheer undertreatment filters light.

The Window Decorating Book

Left: Easy sheers pull back effortlessly with a simple tieback.

Below: Athena draperies are contained when needed but can be released from their ties in order to cover the windows for additional privacy.

(*Above*) Light and dark combine to offer two different looks. (*Below*) Because individuality and expression is key today, multi-toned panels provide a means to make any treatment unique.

(*Above*) At day, let the sun filter gently through sheers; at night, close your draperies all the way for a good nights rest. Hung on a track system, the hardware is quite invisible. (Below) Grommet topped drapery panels, dark and light brown, traverse easily on metal poles.

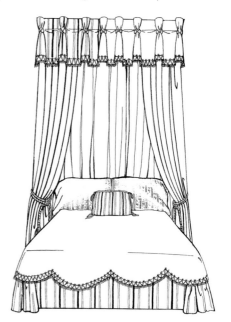

Above: A sheer swag, stationary drapery panels and sheer undertreatment combine.

Left: Golden stationary drapery panels cinched with generous tassels, with sheer undertreatment, are a wonderful way to welcome the day.

Below: Goblet pleated valance with trimmed edge; lush draperies and matching dust ruffle and pillow.

Precise pleats cover a window wall, allowing privacy when needed but gliding open to allow both egress areas to be accessed. Design by Sarah Barnard, Sarah Barnard Designs

Design by Barbara Elliott/Jennifer Ward Woods, Interiors by Decorating Den; photo by Jeff Sanders

(*Above*) Precious butterfly pleats hang quickly with gold clips. (*Below*) Fan pleated draperies hook into a small ring attached to the bottom of the larger drapery ring. The colors and patterning are a popular choice.

Design by Gloria Hill, Interiors by Decorating Den; photo by Randy Foulds

Design by Lisa Landry, Interiors by Decorating Den; photo by Ken Vaughn

(*Above*) Portieres mix with traditional draperies to offer a simply sumptuous bedroom experience. (Below) While the brown fabric tones are slightly masculine, the ruffled edge accents add a hint of femininity.

Design by Jamie Speroff, Interiors by Decorating Den; photo by Olson Photography LLC

Good to Know

What is it about fabric at the window that makes such a compelling statement? Of course, it can soften the architecture of a room, but it also has the unique ability to accentuate it. Fabric can hide flaws around a window area, trap drafts, shield a room's furnishings from the sun and provide a needed focal point.

It can help to muffle sound, manage to pull all the disparate elements of a room together, provide balance and best of all: bestow beauty.

Curtains are mostly just unlined versions of draperies, a simple single or double layer of fabric that is hemmed and hung from a rod at the top of a window frame. Not all curtains are short but the most recognizable of curtains are those that hit the sill of the window and do not extend to the floor.

Curtains can also be defined as a more "novelty" style treatment, probably due to the fact that you will see them used most often in kitchens, bathrooms and children's bedrooms, where fun cotton patterns incorporating various related motifs are pretty standard. So, by nature, they are always a less formal style of window enhancement.

Draperies are the grand older sister to curtains, all dressed up and ready for a night on the town. They are for formal areas, areas in need of lush accents and also employ complicated stitching and multiple layers.

Draperies are the kind of window treatment that you invest heartily in and expect to keep on the windows for multiple years.

While some draperies can be lightweight, such as if they are made of silk, many will be constructed of heavier materials such as velvet, jacquard, satin, matelassé and damask.

And, if they are made of a lighter material, you will more than likely see that the "beauty" material has been lined at least once, if not twice or even three times. You will find more information on these types of linings on page 58.

What follows are specifications for a series of popular curtain and drapery styles, as well as information on a variety of other related topics. Of course, I am only scratching the surface of these remarkable treatments. You have seen many others throughout the pages of this book.

Standard Custom Workmanship & Quality Features

- Double wrapped headings
- 4" or 5" permanent buckram headings (unless "slouched, no buckram" heading requested)
- Pleating is custom tacked with extra thread
- All seems serged and overlocked
- All draperies perfectly matched & table sized
- Blind stitched bottom and side hems. Chain weights may be necessary to prevent billowing in lightweight fabrics.
- Double wrapped 4" or 5" bottom hems and 1½" double side hems
- All draperies weighted at corners and seams.
- Multiple width draperies are placed so that joining seams are hidden behind pleats

Drapery Terminology

- *Width* is one strip of material of any length that can be pleated to a finished dimension across the TOP of between 16" and 24". For example, using a 48" wide material, a width that finishes to 24" is considered double fullness, or 2 to 1; a 16" finished width is considered triple fullness, or 3 to 1. Any number of widths can be joined together to properly cover the window area.
- *Panel* is a single drapery unit of one or more widths which is used specifically for one way (o/w) draw, stack left or stack right and/or stationary units.
- *Pair* is two equal panels that cover a desired area — unless an offset pair is necessary.
- *Return* is the measurement from the rod to the wall; in other words, the projection.
- *Overlap* is the measurement, when draperies are fully closed, of the right leading edge and the left leading edge overlapping each other. This helps balance the pleats and reduce light seepage.

Options Available on Draperies

(see appendices for more options):

- Pinch pleated with 4" or 5" buckram
- Box pleated or box pleated with tabs for rod. Add diameter of rod to finished length. For flat tab draperies use 2 to 1 fullness.
- Rod pocket, gathered (shirred), goblet, flounced, blouson or cuffed.
- Self-lined, inter-lined or lined with polyester-cotton, black-out or thermal suede.

Pleat Spacing

Pleat spacing varies according to the widths of material used to achieve a specified finished width. For example, three widths of material pleated to 59" to the pair will not have the same pleat spacing as three widths of material pleated to 72" to the pair. If the pleats and pleat spacing are to look alike on draperies of different widths, you should specify "comparable fullness" when you order custom draperies. Vertically striped fabrics will not fabricate to allow an identical stripe to fall between pleats.

Ordering Custom Draperies

Since "made-to-measure" draperies are to your exact specifications, measurements must be made with the greatest care and with a steel tape only. Double check all measurements for accuracy — it is often more expensive to remake draperies than make new ones! Measure each window separately even if they appear to be the same size. If length varies, use the shortest length, especially for ceiling to floor length. If this rule is not followed a portion of the drapery may drag on the floor.

Drapery Width (see page 102 for more details)

- Measure width of drapery rod from end to end.
- Add 12" to this figure to include the allowance for standard traverse rod returns and overlap.
- Standard returns are 3" in depth. For over-draperies allow for 6" clearance of under-treatment..
- When ordering panels that draw o/w (one-way), specify which direction: left or right.

Drapery Length

- Measure from top of rod, to floor, to carpet.
- Under-treatment should be at least ½" shorter than overtreatment.
- When floor-length draperies are used, it is best to measure the length at each side and in the center. Use the shortest figure for your measurements (as mentioned above).
- Rod should be placed a minimum of 4" above the window so that hooks and pleats will not be visible from the outside.
- If sill-length, allow 4" below sill so that the bottom hem will not be visible from the outside.
- When using pole rings, measure length from bottom of rings.

Yardage Chart

Yardage Chart for 4" or 5" heading FL (finished length) plus 20", plain fabrics only
Total number of widths per pair or panel

Finished length ↓

	2W	3W	4W	5W	6W	7W	8W	9W	10W	11W	12W	13W	14W	15W
36"	3¼	4¾	6¼	7¾	9¼	10¾	12¼	13¾	15¼	16¾	18¼	19¾	21¼	22¾
40"	3½	5	6½	8	9½	11	12½	14	15½	17	18½	20	21½	23
44"	3¾	5½	7¼	9	10¾	12½	14¼	16	17¾	19½	21¼	23	24¾	26½
48"	4	5¾	7½	9¼	11	12¾	14½	16¼	18	19¾	21½	23¼	25	26¾
52"	4	6	8	10	12	14	16	18	20	22	24	26	28	30
56"	4¼	6½	8½	10¾	12¾	15	16¾	19	21¼	23¼	25½	27½	29¾	31¾
60"	4½	6¾	9	11¼	13½	15¾	18	20	22¼	24½	26¾	29	31¼	33½
64"	4¾	7	9½	11¾	14	16½	18¾	21	23½	25¾	28	30½	32¾	35
68"	5	7½	10	12¼	14¾	17¼	19¾	22	24½	27	29½	32	34¼	36¾
72"	5¼	7¾	10¼	13	15½	18	20½	23	25¾	28¼	30¾	33¼	36	38½
76"	5½	8	10¾	13½	16	18¾	21½	24	26¾	29½	32	34¾	37½	40
80"	5¾	8½	11¼	14	16¾	19½	22¼	25	28	30¾	33½	36¼	39	41¾
84"	6	8¾	11¾	14½	17½	20¼	23¼	26	29	32	34¾	37¾	40½	43½
88"	6	9	12	15	18	21	24	27	30	33	36	39	42	45
92"	6¼	9½	12½	15¾	18¾	22	25	28	31¼	34¼	37½	40½	43¾	46¾
96"	6½	9¾	13	16¼	19½	22¾	26	29	32¼	35½	38¾	42	45¼	48½
100"	6¾	10	13½	16¾	20	23½	26¾	30	33½	36¾	40	43½	46¾	50
104"	7	10½	14	17¼	20¾	24¼	27¾	31	34½	38	41½	45	48¼	51¾
108"	7¼	10¾	14¼	18	21½	25	28½	32	35¾	39¼	42¾	46¼	50	53½

Pleat-to-Fullness Chart

(48" fabric) 2½ times fullness

Pleat to	19	38	57	76	95	114	133	152	171	190	209	228	247	266	285
Widths	1	2	3	4	5	6	7	8	9	10	11	12	13	14	15

(48" fabric) 3 times fullness

Pleat to	15	30	45	60	75	90	105	120	135	150	165	180	195	210	225
Widths	1	2	3	4	5	6	7	8	9	10	11	12	13	14	15

(54" fabric) 2½ times fullness

Pleat to	21	42	63	84	105	126	147	168	189	210	231	254	273	294	315
Widths	1	2	3	4	5	6	7	8	9	10	11	12	13	14	15

(54" fabric) 3 times fullness

Pleat to	17	34	51	68	85	102	119	136	153	170	187	204	221	238	255
Widths	1	2	3	4	5	6	7	8	9	10	11	12	13	14	15

General Calculations

(for detailed terms and information see page 102)

With drapery calculations, one must consider the following: width and length of window, area to be covered, amount of fullness desired, width and type of fabric, allowances for hems and headings, and pattern repeat, if applicable. And after obtaining accurate measurements proceed with the following steps.

Step 1:

Determine the number of the fabric widths required. This is calculated by multiplying the width of the area to be covered by the given fullness factor (listed on the drapery treatment page). Divide this by the by the width of the fabric being used. The result is the number of widths of fabric that are required to achieve the desired fullness. Since fabric suppliers will not sell a part of the width, this figure must be a whole number.

Step 2a:

Calculate the yardage. Add to the length of the treatment, the allowances for hems, headings and where applicable, styling allowances, such as cuffs or blouson tops (such as image below). These allowances are listed on the item page under the corresponding yardage calculation. Next, multiply these amounts by

the number of widths required and divide by 36 to obtain the number of yards. This calculation applies only to solid fabrics or to fabrics that have a pattern repeat of less than six inches. (*Or, to calculate the yardage for a fabric with a pattern repeat of more than six inches.*)

Step 2b:

Add the length and applicable allowances together and divide by the pattern repeat. This figure is the number of pattern repeats that are required to achieve the desired length. If this number is a fraction it must be rounded upward to the nearest whole number.

Step 2c:

Determine the cut length — this is the actual length that the workroom will cut the fabric after allowing for pattern repeats, hems cuffs, puddling, etc. Multiply the number of repeats required by the size of the pattern repeat. This number is the cut length.

Step 2d:

Multiply the number of widths required, as calculated in Step 1, by the cut length. Divide by 36 to obtain the total yardage required for a pattern repeat.

Special Note:

Every attempt has been made to ensure the accuracy of the calculations and yardage charts of the items in this book; however, variations in fabrics or workroom specifications may require certain modifications to the yardage calculations. For complex or elaborate style treatments such as swags, cascades and arched treatments please consult a designer or professional drapery workroom.

Please also note that the photographs and illustrations accompanying each set of yardage calculations are not for the images shown. These images are for illustrative purposes only.

Triple blouson tops on the drapery panels draw the eye with their unique beauty.

Drapery Terms and Calculations Chart

Bishop's Sleeve Minimum length = Add 15" to 20" per pouf.

CD = Cascade Drop. Length of cascades. Usually 3/5 of the undertreatment is most visually pleasing.

CL = Cut Length. The length of fabric to be cut, including allowance for headings, hems and specialty items such as bishop sleeves or cuffs.

C/O = Center opening drapery.

F = Fullness. Fullness after pleating or gathering of drapery; usually 2x for flat panel or tabbed draperies, 2.5x for pinch or box pleated and 3x for sheers

FL = Finished Length. The length of pairs or panels before adding for headings and hems (what the finished length of the drapery will be after fabrication).

Fullness Minimum = To be considered "custom" draperies usually need 2½ to 3x fullness. Sheers require triple fullness.

FW = Finished Width. The total width of a pair or panel of draperies including returns and overlap.

HH = Heading and Hem allowance. Custom draperies require doubling wrapping the heading and hems. Therefore, you must add 16" for a drapery with 4" headings and hems and 20" for a drapery with 5" heading and hem.

OL = Overlap(s). 6" per pair of single hung (no sheers) draperies and 3.5x" for single hung panel.

O/W = Single panel, one-way drapery.

Puddle panels = Add 6" to 18" to the FL (finished length)

R = Repeat. The total inches before a pattern repeats itself..

RFW = Rod Face Width, the total rod width, not including return to the wall

RT = Return(s). Rod projection from wall. Add 6" (3" for each side) for standard single hung draperies and 12" for double hung (over sheers) draperies. *Example*: A 102" Rod (RFW) single hung pair of draperies would require an additional 12". 6" for returns to the wall and 6" for overlap. A double hung pair of draperies would require an additional 18". 12" for returns to wall and 6" for OL.

SB = Stack-back. The amount fabric that stacks back when you open the pair or panel of draperies, usually one-third of the rod face.

SBGC = Stack-back with full glass clearance = rod face x 1.5.

SD = Swag Drop. Using the rule of fifths (ratios of 5 or 6 are more pleasing to the eye), swag drop should equal about one-fifth of the length of the undertreatment.

TW = Total Width. The total width of drapery fabric required after multiplying the fabric widths required.

TY = Total Yardage. Total yardage required.

Try it! = Calculate based on a 70" RFW (rod face width) and 84" FL (finished length) single hung, center opening drapery.
70" RFW + 12" for RT & OL (returns and overlap) = 82" FW (finished width). 82 x 2.5 = 205 TW (total width). 205 ÷ 54 (width of fabric used) = 3.79. Round to the next whole number because fabric stores do not sell half widths of fabric.

Now figure the length. 84" FL + 16" HH (heading and hem allowance) = 100" CL (cut length).

Now multiply 4 (fabrics widths required) x 100" (CL) for a total of 400". 400" ÷ 36 = 11.1 (total yards required). Always round this number up to the next whole number, in this case 12. It's always good for the workroom to have a little extra fabric to work with.

Refer back to this page when using calculations on the succeeding pages.

Pinch (French) Pleat

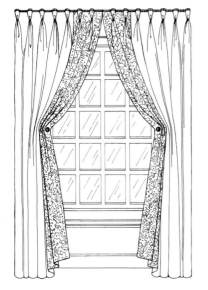

Photo: Pinch pleat; *illustration:* goblet pleat

This very traditional panel drapery is topped with a series of narrow, "pinched" folds. Also called "French" pleats, this type of drapery requires a good bit of stackback space, as pinching the top of the fabric results in a greater fabric fullness at the bottom.

For additional treatments and embellishments, see Appendices beginning on page 288.

Yardage *(including Pinch Pleat, Goblet, Cartridge, Bell, Euro and Fan pleated)*

Step 1 – RFW (rod face width) + 12" for RT & OL (returns and overlap) x 2.5 or 3.0 ÷ width of fabric = number of widths required (round up to whole number) Three times fullness is recommended for very light weight fabrics such as silk

Step 2a – FL (finished length) + 16" for HH (headings and hems) x widths required ÷ 36 = yardage (round up to whole number) without pattern repeat (*or*)

Step 2b – FL (finished length) + 16" for HH ÷ pattern repeat = number of repeats required (round up to whole number)

Step 2c – Number of repeats x pattern repeat = CL (cut length)

Step 2d – Number of widths x CL (cut length) ÷ 36 = yardage with pattern repeat (round up to whole number)

Things to Consider
> Alternate lining color
> Center opening or one way panel
> What type of rod?
> Tiebacks required?

Special Notes
1. A check measure is recommended for all full length draperies.
2. See page 102 for detailed calculating terms.

Photo: Smocked pleat; *illustration:* pencil pleat

This very attractive heading exhibits even gathers across the width of the curtain or drape to great feminine appeal.

For additional treatments and embellishments, see Appendices beginning on page 288.

Yardage *(including Pencil, Smocked Accordion and Shirred Cuff)*

Step 1 – RFW (rod face width) + 6" for RT (returns) x 2.5 or 3.0 ÷ width of fabric = number of widths required (round up to whole number) Three times fullness recommended for very light weight fabrics such as silks and sheers

Step 2a – FL (finished length) + 16" for HH (headings and hems) x widths required ÷ 36 = yardage (round up to whole number) without pattern repeat (*or*)

Step 2b – FL (finished length) + 16" for HH ÷ pattern repeat = number of repeats required (round up to whole number)

Step 2c – Number of repeats required x pattern repeat = cut length

Step 2d – Number of widths x CL (cut length) ÷ 36 = yardage with pattern repeat (round up to whole number)

Things to Consider

> Alternate lining color

> Tiebacks required?

> Center opening or one way panel

Special Notes

1. A check measure is recommended for all full length draperies.

2. Smocked treatments should stay stationary due to the nature of the header.

3. See page 102 for detailed calculating terms

Photo & illustration: Tab top

This simple style has been popular for many years, as it has many options for decoration and also celebrates the beauty of the rod that it hangs from.

For additional treatments and embellishments, see Appendices beginning on page 288.

Yardage *(including Tab, Gathered Tab, Pleated Tab and Ties)*

Step 1 – RFW (rod face width) + 6" for RT (returns) x 2 ÷ width of fabric = number of widths required (round up to whole number) Two and a half times fullness is recommended for very light weight fabrics such as silks and sheers

Step 2a – FL (finished length) + 20" for HH (headings and hems) x widths required ÷ 36 = yardage (round up to whole number) without pattern repeat *(or)*

Step 2b – FL (finished length) + 20" for HH ÷ pattern repeat = number of repeats required (round up to whole number)

Step 2c – Number of repeats x pattern repeat = CL (cut length)

Step 2d – Number of widths x CL (cut length) ÷ 36 = yardage with pattern repeat (round up to whole number)

Things to Consider

> Alternate lining color
> What type of rod?
> Center opening or one way panel

Special Notes

1. Yardage calculations include tabs.
2. Only 2 times fullness is required on this treatment to obtain the proper effect.
3. See page 102 for detailed calculating terms

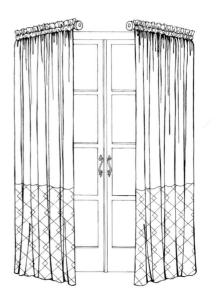

Photo: Unembellished rod pocket; *illustration:* rod pocket with ruffled top

This treatment has a pocket at the top through which a rod for hanging is inserted. It can be dressed with a ruffle above the rod and also, depending upon the amount of fabric used, create a "shirred" effect.

For additional treatments and embellishments, see Appendices beginning on page 288.

Yardage *(including Rod Pocket, Double Rod Pocket, Rod Pocket with Standup and Rod Pocket with Belt Loops)*

Step 1 – RFW (rod face width) + 6" for RT (returns, if used) x 2.5 or 3.0 ÷ width of fabric = number of widths required (round up to whole number). 3x fullness is recommended for very light weight fabrics such as silks and sheers ÷ 36 = yardage without pattern repeat

Step 2a – FL (finished length) + 16" for HH (headings and hems) x widths required ÷ 36 = yardage (round up to whole number) without pattern repeat *(or)*

Step 2b – FL + 16" for HH ÷ pattern repeat = number of repeats required (round up to whole number)

Step 2c – Number of repeats x pattern repeat = CL (cut length)

Step 2d – Number of widths x CL (cut length) ÷ 36 = yardage with pattern repeat (round up to whole number)

Things to Consider

> Alternate lining color
> Center opening or one way panel
> What type of rod and tiebacks?
> Ruffle or frill needed on top of treatment?

Special Notes

1. This is a stationary treatment but can be moved with some difficulty — not recommended.
2. This treatment cannot be used when the treatment underneath is mounted up at the ceiling.
3. See page 102 for detailed calculating terms

Box Pleated

Photo: Rod mounted box pleat; *illustration*: Board-mounted box pleat

Crisp folds that resemble the corners of a box are the hallmark of this tailored drapery treatment.

For additional treatments and embellishments, see Appendices beginning on page 288.

Yardage *(including Box pleated, Inverted Box Pleat)*

Step 1 – RFW (rod face width) + 12" for RT and OL (returns and overlap) x 2.5 or 3 ÷ width of fabric = number of widths required (round up to whole number) Use 2.5 fullness if using a traverse rod

Step 2a – FL (finished length) + 16" for HH (headings and hems) x widths required ÷ 36 = yardage (round up to whole number) without pattern repeat *(or)*

Step 2b – FL (finished length) + 16" for HH ÷ pattern repeat = number of repeats required (round up to whole number)

Step 2c – Number of repeats x pattern repeat = CL (cut length)

Step 2d – Number of widths x CL (cut length) ÷ 36 = yardage with pattern repeat (round up to whole number)

Things to Consider

> Alternate lining color
> Center opening or one way panel
> What type of rod, if any? This treatment can also be mounted on a board
> Tiebacks required?

Special Notes

1. A check measure is recommended for all full length draperies.
2. Reduce fullness to 2.5 if using a traverse rod.
3. See page 102 for detailed calculating terms

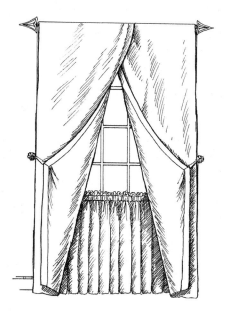

Photo & illustration: Tent fold

A tuxedo drapery is more about the mid-section of the treatment than the header as its most recognizable aspect is the way it folds back to reveal a contrast lining.

For additional treatments and embellishments, see Appendices beginning on page 288.

Yardage *(including Tuxedo, Tent Fold and Stationary Flat Panel)*

Step 1 – RFW (rod face width) + 10" for RT and OL (returns and overlap, if used) ÷ width of fabric = number of widths required (round up to whole number)

Step 2a – FL (finished length) + 12" for HH (headings and hems) x widths required ÷ 36 = yardage (round up to whole number) without pattern repeat (*or*)

Step 2b – FL (+ 12" for HH ÷ pattern repeat = number of repeats required (round up to whole number)

Step 2c – Number of repeats x pattern repeat = CL (cut length)

Step 2d – Number of widths x CL (cut length) ÷ 36 = yardage with pattern repeat (round up to whole number)

Step 3 – Calculate with same formula for contrast lining

Step 4 – Allow 1/2 yard for ties; 1 yard for larger sash ties

Things to Consider

> Alternate lining color

> What type of rod?

> Center opening or one way panel

Special Notes

1. Large returns are not recommended.

2. Tuxedo draperies limit the amount of light entering the room.

3. Not recommended for windows that are proportionately wider than high.

4. See page 102 for detailed calculating terms

Photo: Clip-hung, traversing Athena; *illustration:* stationary Athena

This type of treatment is created from a simple flat panel with generously-spaced rings or clips to attach it to the rod, as well as offer an almost swagged effect at the heading. This type of treatment usually puddles.

For additional treatments and embellishments, see Appendices beginning on page 288.

Yardage *(including Athena, Flat Panel)*

Step 1 – RFW (rod face width) + 12" for RT (returns) x 2 or 2.5 ÷ width of fabric = number of widths required (round up to whole number) Two and one half fullness is recommended for very light weight fabrics such as silks and sheers

Step 2a – FL (finished length) + 16" for HH (headings and hems) x widths required ÷ 36 = yardage (round up to whole number) without pattern repeat (*or*)

Step 2b – FL + 16" for HH ÷ pattern repeat = number of repeats required (round up to whole number)

Step 2c – Number of repeats x pattern repeat = CL (cut length)

Step 2d – Number of widths x CL (cut length) ÷ 36 = yardage with pattern repeat (round up to whole number)

Things to Consider

> Alternate lining color

> What type of rod, ring and clip?

> Center opening or one way panel?

Special Notes

1. A puddle of 6" has been allowed in the yardage. If more is desired, add to length + allowance.
2. Soft, drapeable fabrics are recommended.
3. For self or contrast facing, allow 1/4 yard per width
4. Lining or contrast lining equals drapery yardage
5. See page 102 for detailed calculating terms

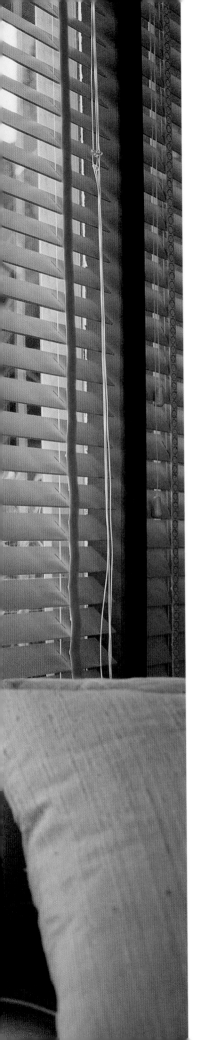

Blinds

There is something in the structured simplicity of a blind that appeals universally. Neat, compact and orderly, horizontal and vertical blinds fulfill a multitude of needs with the simple pull of a cord or twist of a wand. Consisting of a

head rail system, slats, louvers or vanes and (with horizontals) a bottom to finish, blinds can interface with any interior due to the wide range of colors, materials, stains and decorative tapes and cord weights. Fit them inside the window to lie flush with the frame or mount them outside the frame, blinds are infinitely capable of being beautiful and functional.

Left: Two inch wood blinds in a beige tone with complementary sky blue decorative tape have classic appeal while controlling light and maintaining privacy.

Above: Wood blinds below arched window.

History in the Making

While blinds have been premier window coverings within this lifetime, it is worth mentioning that they have been around for much longer. Egyptian culture has record of the use of vertical blinds, constructed of reeds. Apparently, slaves were instructed to pour water over the porous material, in an effort to cool the rooms of their masters. Additionally, woven bamboo blinds in ancient China were employed to filter light in palaces and huts. Subsequently, they evolved into shutters, which in turn became wood slat blinds. You will find record of the use of blinds in America as early as the mid-1700s.

In 1841, a U.S. patent was awarded to New Orleans' John Hampson, who invented a method of adjusting the angle of slats in a Venetian blind.

The 1930s and 1940s saw two-inch Venetian blinds in most every home and office in America, but due to the lack of anti-static properties and their cumbersome nature, they were difficult to clean and not terribly pretty.

It wasn't until modern technology came into play in the mid-twentieth century that vertical and horizontal blinds truly burgeoned. Processes for casting aluminum into strips, developed in the mid-1940s, was the beginning. Yet for our modern world, we can look to the 1960s and 1970s, as circa World War II draperies began to age on their rods, that the call for blinds was truly heard. By the 1980s, mass production and thus, the use of hard window treatments in interiors were common. The sleek lines and simple manipulation of slats to control light and privacy, so modern, showed fabric treatments the door.

Two-inch aluminum slat blinds offer modern beauty and superior lift mechanisms.

Today's Blinds

Today, horizontal and vertical blinds are still enjoying their place in interiors all over the world. Wider slats, replicating the look of shutters, to vertical blinds—a virtual moveable curtain wall—offer plentiful choices. Versatile, uncomplicated and clean, their colorways are generous, wood and faux wood products are unbelievably hard to discern from one another and blinds work in tandem with the escalating trend toward fabric at the windows. A new hybrid, too, basically a horizontal or vertical slat meets fabric, combine for a softened window appearance. Offering an attractive horizontal and/or vertical line from not just the interior but also the exterior of the home, the uniformity of these window treatments is attractive and suitable for any interior.

The fabric/vane combination is technically a shade system, but due to its tilt function (especially) which is inherently more like a blind, this unique product bridges the gap between blinds and shades.

Horizontal Blinds

Horizontal blinds most often come to mind when considering the best method for covering a window, because they fulfill so many of the basic requirements, as well as offer a sleek, modern appearance and a low to moderate price point. Easy to acquire, fast turnaround and a wide variety of materials and slat sizes make horizontal blinds a perennial favorite. And better yet, their solid construction makes this a window treatment that will last and last.

Above: Simple wood blinds provide a clean, modern look.

Right top: The Plantation shutter blind combines the elegant look of a plantation shutter with the ease and function of a blind. The 2½" "shutter louver" slat ensures a clear view through when open and complete light control when closed.

Right bottom: Beige decorative tape enhances the look of these horizontal blinds, harmonizing well with the coordinating stripe in the top treatment.

The Facts: Horizontal Blinds

Advantages: Can control light direction by a simple twist of the slats; will harmonize with just about any type of soft treatment; can be motorized in a variety of manners; typically a fast turnaround for this kind of product; routless construction offers the ultimate privacy; hidden brackets and no valance options allow this blind to almost disappear into the inner window frame; cordless operating systems make treatments safer for children and pets

Disadvantages: Rout holes in the center of a blind will allow anyone interested to see inside your home. Be certain you buy a blind with rout holes placed at the back of the slat—or opt for the new "no hole" construction; dust will accumulate, even with a built-in dust repellant; metal blinds can bend and clank against a window when a breeze enters the room

Cost: An inexpensive vinyl product can be had for about $10 but if you are looking for a treatment that will last, expect to spend at least $50 per 30" x 42" window. As always, extras, such as valances and various blind materials such as wood, faux wood, aluminum, etc. will cause great price fluctuation.

Lifespan: Decades

Most Appropriate Locations: Any window will do, although some materials are not suitable for some areas (such as wood blinds in a bathroom). Also note that any treatment near a stove where there is airborne grease will be difficult to clean. Think about raising your blind fully when cooking to avoid coating the slats, which will in turn attract dust.

Care & Cleaning: Most blind slats are now anti-static and dust repellant, though some more than others. Clean the slats with a feather duster to remove weekly accumulation of residue. You can also have blinds cleaned sonically through a take down, clean and reinstall service that cleans blinds thoroughly with no damage or wear.

Left: The horizontal stripe of the blinds plays off the vertical stripe of the box pleat top treatments. Design by Judy Underwood & Cliff Welles, Interiors by Decorating Den

Above: The design of these room darkening blinds provides tighter slat closure with concealed cord routing holes. The unique two-inch slats interlock to seal out incoming light, increase privacy and provide additional security.

Below: Tilt cords flank the left side of this horizontal blind; lift cords are on the right. Using the same type of hand mechanisms on both sides allows a more symmetrical look, although tilt wands are also very popular. With a continuous cord loop system for lifting, even the heaviest wood blinds feel lighter.

Blinds

Two and ⅜" wood blinds offer an almost unobstructed view when they are open, being there is more space between the slats. The larger slat is also a cost-effective alternative to the plantation shutter. Notice how well the pecan finish blends with the cabinetry. This sleek look is a knock-out in a modern but warm kitchen.

This 100 percent basswood two-inch blind with chocolate decorative tapes and vintage bronze hardware offers a 100 percent eco-friendly UV finish.

It looks like natural wood, but it isn't, which is just what you need for areas of high moisture where the potential for warpage and cracking exist.

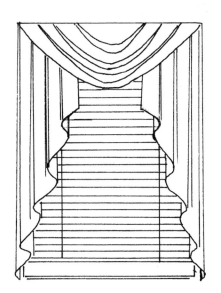

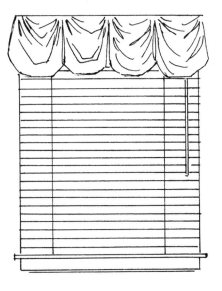

Arched gathered valance over wood Venetian blinds; Fabric draped swag over blinds; Balloon valance over wood blinds

Vertical Blinds

Neat and elegant vertical blinds can cover a large expanse of glass, such as a sliding glass door or large picture window, easily. With individual stiffened cloth or vinyl (typically) louvers that can rotate 180 degrees as well as pull completely out of the way, vertical blinds are a terrific way to obtain coverage similar to that of a drapery, but with a better capability to control light. Best yet, vertical blinds can strengthen a room's focus with their strong lines and elongated structure. Beautiful colors abound, with embossed prints to fit any décor; custom valances (upholstered and wood, to name a few) to provide a pop of trendy beauty; and the vanes themselves are available from a sheer, translucent material to the hard edge of aluminum. And now, many manufacturers are creating soft fabric verticals (sheer fabric adjoining each vane), which replicate the look of draperies but offer the flexibility of a typical vertical blind.

Previous page:
Above left: The long, narrow nature of these individual windows is prime territory for vertical blinds. It was a good decision to cover each window individually rather than fill the wall with one large blind, which would only serve to overpower the rest of the setting.
Below left: Floor length fabric swagged on shirred rod over vertical blinds; Swag with ruffled side drops over vertical blinds.

This page:
Above Vertical blinds are an exceptional choice in this dining area, emphasizing the vertical nature of the wall paneling. Try to picture horizontal blinds now. Exactly. They wouldn't be right in this setting. The choice is clearly vertical.

The Facts: Vertical Blinds

Advantages: Can cover large expanses of glass; newer styles hang perfectly straight without any weights or bottom chains; operating systems are now quiet and smooth; some manufacturers boast over 80 colors available; can be motorized in a variety of manners; its elongated structure will augment the height of a room; allows good air circulation; some verticals have the capability of slipping strips of material (such as wallpaper) into the vanes to match a room's décor

Disadvantages: Cheaper vertical blind slats will clank and tangle together; hardware is visible without a headrail (be sure to order one); they're kid magnets (hide and seek has never been more enticing!); perception still puts them in a corporate rather than a residential setting; can be imposing in a room

Cost: Prices can vary depending upon the material selected, but a very simple version approximately seven foot tall by about five foot wide will cost around $100.

Lifespan: Decades

Most Appropriate Locations: For areas with great expanses of glass, such as sliding glass doors, as well as tall casement windows, large picture windows, arch-top and some angular windows.

Care & Cleaning: Minimum maintenance. Blind slats are now anti-static and dust repellant, though some more than others. Clean the vanes with a feather duster to remove weekly accumulation of residue. You can also have blinds cleaned sonically through a take down, clean and reinstall service that cleans blinds thoroughly with no damage or wear.

Left: This is a setting in which vertical fabric/vane blinds work perfectly — covering large expanses of glass. Consider opting for a split draw so that you have equal stackback on either side of the window, versus a large, potentially clumsy stackback on just one side.

Above: Vertical blinds work well when used in conjuction with sliding glass doors.

Good to Know: Blinds

- Consider cordless blinds, those that raise and lower with slight pressure applied to the bottom rail, for homes with children and pets. Easy to lift, they provide a sleek, modern look and the issue of safety will never arise again.

- For vibrant color, consider metal blinds. The color application on metal is bright, tough and can withstand plenty of abuse. They are also available cordless.

- Generally, the smaller the slat, the less light leakage when shut. Micro mini blinds are a great option in areas that require total darkness.

- If your goal is to enhance architectural details or create a focal point, wood blinds with a quality stained or painted finish will offer a sense of permanence.

- Be sure to select blinds treated with an anti-static finish to alleviate dust build-up.

- Consider vertical blinds if your goal is to enhance the height of a room. The vertical nature will make a low ceiling look higher.

- With vertical blinds, be sure to allow about ¾" clearance from the floor to allow for ease when traversing. Also, it is important to note that when the vertical blind has been pulled to the side, there will be stackback — i.e., a small amount of vertically stacked product — that will remain, as there is no headrail for a vertical blind to escape into.

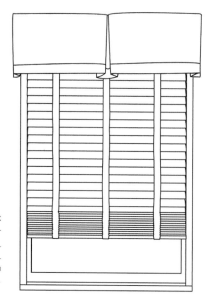

Right: Banded, box pleated valance over wood blinds. Custom rendering by DreamDraper® design software, www.dreamdraper.com © 2009 Evan Marsh Designs, Inc.

(*Above*) One and a half inch pine wood blinds with black decorative tape is a great look on French doors, fitting neatly under the door's handle. The classic valance topper finishes the look well.

Blinds

Left: Solid wood vertical blinds are available as either a one way draw (the vanes pull either to the left or right only) or as a split draw, in which the vanes separate in the middle of the treatment and pull half one way and half the opposite diirection. Remember that there will be some stackback once the vanes are pulled to the side and to allow at least ¾" clearance from the floor for easy traversing.

Middle: Beige wood blinds with tone-on-tone decorative tape exhibit a cozy, warm feeling in this sitting room.

Right: Two-inch wood blinds with decorative tape and valance perfectly complement the patterned wallcovering and are enough of a window covering that the arched window can remain uncovered. An elegant, stylish look.

The Window Decorating Book

Above left: The head rail of this horizontal blind treatment is hidden by the addition of a soft handkerchief valance. Who would have thought blinds could be so ultimately feminine?

Design by Judith Slaughter, Interiors by Decorating Den

Below left: The simple sophistication of neutral tones is heightened by the clean lines of horizontal blinds.

Below right: Punches of mauve and olive oil hues couple with warm gray walls and clean horizontal blinds to bring a fresh versatility to this dining room.

This page, below: A majestic focal point is enhanced by the addition of whimsical drapery panels and horizontal blinds. The colors in this room are absolutely enchanting—while using some of the most popular colors of today, they are used sparingly. And isn't less always more?

Design by Judith Slaughter, Interiors by Decorating Den

This page, right: A cloud shade over a wood blind, with decorative rod and finials.

Allow just a little bit of morning sunshine to enter the bathroom with the blinds open just a crack.

A clean and consistent look is provided by one-inch slat wood blinds.

The Window Decorating Book

Using blinds as a way to make offices private are also perfect for times when no privacy is necessary.

Sleek aluminum blinds look ultra sharp in a modern setting.

Shades

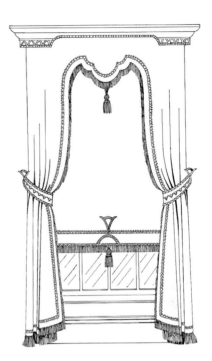

Alone or as a dramatic accompaniment to another treatment, shades come in all shapes and configurations. Clean edged and neat, shades can take a back seat to beautiful architectural details when up and out of the way, or add stunning emphasis. Best, they are typically an economical alternative to draperies, providing the beauty of fabric (such as with soft shades), with less volume yardage. Plus, in areas where full-length draperies are not practical, shades are ultimately suited.

Consider, also, "hard" shades, capable of fitting into awkward areas, inaccessible windows (such as skylights) and even used as unique room dividers.

Left: Casual Roman shades with blueberry banding help tie the room's blue and white motif together. It is the simplicity of the design that makes this room so cohesive: the large color patches combine well with the stripes and patterns, making this an inviting and comfortable interior.

Above: Fringed Roman shade under cornice and drapery panels.

History in the Making

As you may have suspected, shades have long been known for their function — to protect the home from damaging solar heat and to provide privacy. At first appearing as a piece of fabric stretched over some kind of wooden frame, it was attached to the window and was also sometimes hinged. Evolving into draped fabric, the shade pulled up and out of the way with a simple cord system, then progressed to the popular, lush balloon shade (among others). The eighteenth century witnessed the invention of the roll-up shade, as well as the Roman shade, with its unique operating system offering folds of fabric from stiff to graceful. Flat shades of that time (such as the roll-up) were decorated with painted scenes and florals. Since then, shades have been a popular part of many an interior.

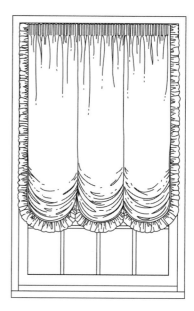

Left: In order to fully appreciate the complexities of a Roman fold shade, one needs to examine it from the side. Beautiful folds of fabric fall together harmoniously; when open, they lie flat and cover the window span thoroughly. With a tug on the chain, the treatment fits neatly into its valance.

Above: Note the decorative ruffled edges, an added enhancement. *Custom rendering by DreamDraper® design software, www.dreamdraper.com © 2009 Evan Marsh Designs, Inc.*

Today's Shades

Today, there are so many shade choices, it's literally staggering. From roller shades to honeycomb to pleated to woven wood to fabric, there's a shade to fit every room. You should first determine whether you want a "hard" shade (categorized primarily by the lack of soft fabric) or a "soft" shade — a shade billowier and more fabric-pretty than stiff. Then, you'll be made in the shade! Take your time, consider your options, analyze your needs and plan how you want your new shade to fit into your décor.

Pretty sheer fabric makes a unique flat fold Roman shade, allowing the sweeping view to filter through while shielding furnishings from UV rays. This is the kind of beauty treatment that is more about enhancing a décor than providing privacy.

The Facts: "Hard" Shades

Advantages: Bottom Up/Top Down features in some applications add to the flexibility, such as in areas like bath and bedrooms; can work in difficult areas such as skylights, angled windows and arches; option of cordless draw makes shades a good choice for safety; inside or outside mount on window frame; multiple shades can be installed on one headrail

Disadvantages: When closed, there is no capability to manipulate the shade to allow light to filter in; maximum/minimum widths cannot be over or understepped; some arch tops are stationary; woven wood shades are mostly transparent unless they have a privacy backing

Cost: Can vary widely depending upon the type of shade selected

Lifespan: Years+. Technology has vastly improved the mechanisms.

Most Appropriate Locations: Just about any location in the home from a livingroom or den to a bedroom or bathroom.

Care & Cleaning: Depending upon the type, judgment must be used. Wipe clean any flat surface-style shade when needed; use a feather duster on products such as woven woods. Never use water or other cleaning solvent unless specifically mentioned by the manufacturer.

Sweet as honey (comb).

Left: Next time you decorate, consider all of the beautiful colors available to you in honeycomb (cellular) shades. Forego the standard white and try something soothing in a bedroom, for example, such as this tranquil blue.

Above: Cellular shades not only work well in regular double hung windows but also are the perfect choice for skylights, due to their light nature and secure methods of installation.

Below: In egress areas, a light cellular shade is a stylish treatment to employ. Consider, too, the bottom up/top down features such as you see in this example.

Good to Know: Hard & Soft Shade Options

What's right for your situation? Here's a look at your options:

"HARD" SHADES

Accordion: *see* Pleated

Cellular: *see* Honeycomb

Fabric/Vane Combinations: Most of these products are better known by their brand names: Silhouette®, Luminette® and Shangri-La® to name a few. In basic terms, they are vanes between which fabric has been suspended. Closed, these products look like regular shades; open, they look quite like a fabric treatment. With the treatment still in a closed position but with the vanes rotated open, they filter the light, thus allowing more control than a regular shade.

Honeycomb: Named after the cellular shape of the comb of the honeybee, honeycomb shades are a flexible, forgiving material that will accommodate unusually shaped windows. With the option of single, double or triple honeycomb, these cells trap air, making them perfect for homes requiring sound and thermal insulation. Best, they can be installed either horizontally or vertically, and are available in a variety of material weights, from sheer to complete light blockage. Also known as Cellular shades. Honeycombs are available in a variety of sizes: from ⅜" to two inches.

Matchstick blinds: Don't let the name fool you — this is a shade, similar to woven wood and grass shades. Horizontally-placed sticks of toothpick-thin bamboo are woven together and then will fold up in pleats like a Roman shade or operate like a standard shade. Better used in a sun porch area where the issue of sun filtering, rather than privacy, is most important.

Mesh: Synthetic materials of various densities of weave and color options offer a high-tech look. Typically a roll-up, these shades can be motorized to add to their futuristic appeal.

Pleated: A single layer of sturdy fabric with crisp pleats that fold up like an accordion when raised and offer a slight zig-zag look when closed. Fabrics can range from very sheer to totally private and the pleats are usually about one inch in size. Also known as Accordion shades.

Roller: Vinyl or fabric, this shade is operated with a spring or clutch system that rolls up into a tube when open. Today, there are many options to add individual design flourishes to the bottom, including lace, fringe and decorative pulls. Roller shades can be had in anything from sheer to total light blockage, but being a solid piece, can only be so flexible in controlling light. There have been improvements made throughout the years, and the clumsy mechanisms of the past have been replaced with the capability for precise positioning, zero snapback and decorative valances to hide the top of the roller.

Solar: A spectacular tool to control the harmful rays of the sun, solar shades filter and diffuse bright sunlight without sacrificing your view of the out-of-doors. A downside is that most solar shades are not meant to offer privacy, so they are best used in conjunction with another treatment, such as a drapery.

Woven grass/wood: Beautiful blends of wood, bamboo, reeds and grasses make woven shades a natural, warm choice, but they require more stacking space than the thinner honeycomb and pleated shades. Banding options add a beautiful finishing touch. Request a privacy backing if you want them to do more than filter light. *See also* Matchstick blinds.

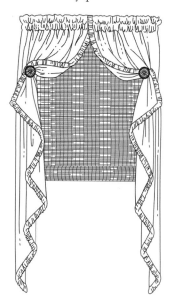

Left: Rod pocket curtains held back with medallions, over woven wood shade.

Woven wood shades in a Roman fold style are the height of fashion in this modern living area where privacy is definitely not an issue.

Shades

SOFT" SHADES

Austrian: A formal treatment that offers shirred, vertical panels (versus the horizontal panels of the Roman shade). Note that this treatment, when installed and/or created improperly, will have a tendency to pull in on the sides.

Balloon: Light and airy, this is a lined (but not interlined) shade made of soft, lightweight fabric. Completely operational, it resembles its cousin, the cloud valance, when open, but offers the operational capability of being able to provide privacy and protection from the sun when closed. Billowy and lush, this is a beautiful fabric treatment that is as close to a full-on drapery treatment as you will get, though it closes vertically, as a normal shade will, and is out of the way when open.

Cloud: This fabric shade has a gathered heading that cascades into soft poufs when opened. Similar to the balloon shade, it can be finished with or without a decorative skirt at the bottom edge.

Roman: This corded shade has rods set horizontally on the backside of the fabric which, when raised, form a series of sideways pleats, usually about four to six inches deep. The beauty of a Roman shade is that it implies the look and feel of drapery, but it raises and lowers horizontally. Can be made with either flat folds or overlapping folds. Not recommended for window applications wider or longer than 84".

Shirred: A traditional Roman shade taken one step further to offer romantic shirring on each of the pleats. An elegant look. For best effect, soft, drapeable fabrics are suggested.

Rod pocket soft specialty shade.

Shades

Some of the more common hard and soft shade styles include:

This page: Accordion/pleated shades look like an accordion when closed and seem to zigzag when open.

Next page:

Upper row, left: A balloon/cloud shade looks soft and billowy, but appears more flat when completely down.

Upper row, middle: A bottom up/top down is moreso a mechanism than an actual shade, with capability to lower the shade from the top or the bottom of the windowsill for specific privacy needs.

Upper row, right: Cellular/honeycomb shades resemble the home of the honeybee, cellular in structure.

Middle row, left: Fabric/vane combinations look like a shade when closed and a fabric treatment when open.

Middle row, middle: Matchstick blinds are thin pieces of wood woven together to create a shading system.

Middle row, right: Roller shades are operated with a spring or clutch system that rolls up into a tube when open.

Lower row, left: Roman shades offer sideways pleats with either flat or overlapping folds of fabric.

Lower row, middle: Sunscreens filter and diffuse light without sacrificing the view.

Lower row, right: Woven wood shades are similar to matchstick blinds and are made of bamboo, reeds and grasses.

Accordion/Pleated

Balloon/Cloud

Bottom Up/Top Down

Cellular/Honeycomb

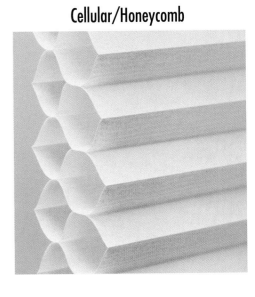

Fabric/Vane Combination

Matchstick

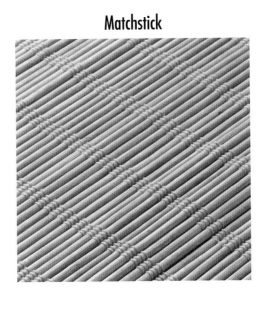

Roller

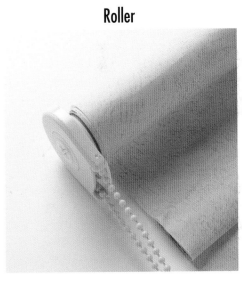

Roman

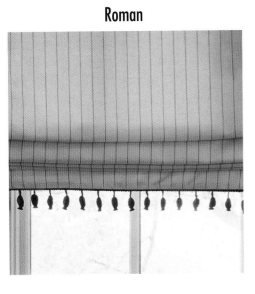

Solar

Woven Wood

The Facts: "Soft" Shades

Advantages: Can often use COM (Customer's Own Material) to coordinate in with existing fabrics; fabric offers a softer look; greater variety of colors and patterns than regular shades; Bottom Up/Top Down features add to the flexibility

Disadvantages: Being fabric, this kind of shade is susceptible to environmental factors such as smoke, sunlight and moisture; material will break down more quickly than some of the hard product shades

Cost: Typically more expensive than a hard shade, being it is often created in a workroom rather than a fabricating facility, soft shades can vary greatly in price depending upon the style. However, a flat fold Roman shade 36" wide by 42" high can cost (minimally) about $400.

Lifespan: About six years, if it is lined properly

Most Appropriate Locations: Any area that needs softening, although fabric is not well suited for areas with high moisture, sun or smoke—especially if not lined.

Care & Cleaning: As with any kind of fabric-style product, consult with either the workroom who created the treatment, or with a professional drapery/shade cleaner. To freshen, you can remove the shade (if you are confident you will be able to rehang it properly) and hang on an outdoor clothesline, or you can vacuum/feather dust.

Left: This tailored Roman shade stacks very neatly due to its crisp pleating system.

Above: This Roman shade enchants with its toile fabric and contrast banding. Roman shades are a lovely means of achieving fabric at a window that cannot accomodate full drapery panels. Crisp and clean, this fabric shade is a true winner.

Left: This Serenade™ Roman-style shade is shown in the classic flat panel style with visual interest heightened by the wood-like fabric, which mimics the natural look of reeds, grasses and bamboo.

Middle: Above a busy prep area, most fabric treatments would be too fussy and involved. With fabric shades, however, such as this Roman beauty, you are allowed softness up and out of the way of your workspace when necessary, and full privacy and sun control at the pull of a cord.

Right: Blackout Roman shades are modern and eye-catching.

The Window Decorating Book

Above left: These bottom up/top down matchstick shades, with warm brown stain and bright white accent threads, showcase the view while providing privacy.

Below left: Flat fold Roman shades in a bottom up/top down style are a brilliant solution for hard to treat French doors. The natural tones are a complementary shoo-in — perfect for blending with woodwork.

Below right: The waterfall shade, which gracefully falls from the top down in a neat, clean cascade, coupled with green contrast fabric banding, is a natural beauty.

This page, below: The basketweave texture on this tabbed hem roller shade enhances the natural décor and complements the wood finial and metal rod accent. The rod accent is a means to draw the shade without touching the shade material (and thus possibly dirtying the fabric through repeated handling).

This page, right: Ring and rod top Roman shade with inverted tab and rod bottom.

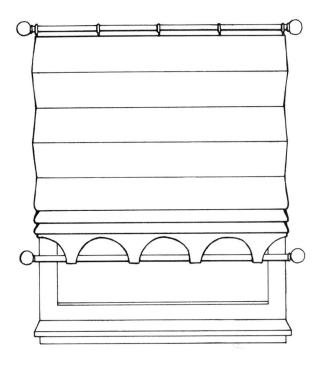

Above: Handwoven grasses and reeds make up this natural shade.

Left: Natural woods and fibers are woven into a Roman-style shade that offers a unique fusion of natural beauty and streamlined style. Long a shade only seen in sun porches, the woven wood shade is fast becoming a beautiful choice for modern homes and offices.

Below: Scarf valance over woven wood shade.

Custom rendering by DreamDraper® design software, www.dreamdraper.com © 2009 Evan Marsh Designs, Inc.

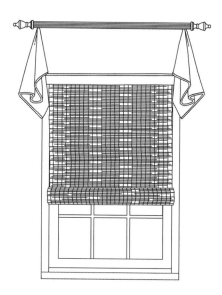

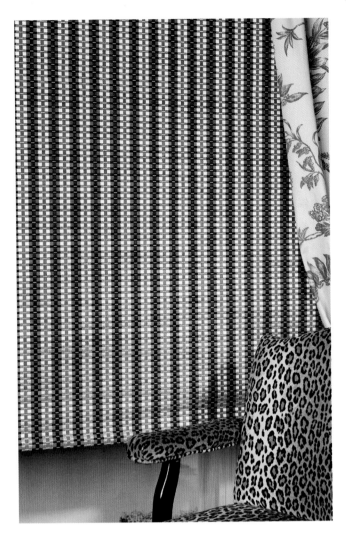

Above: The exotic patterning in this woven wood shade is exceptionally eye-catching and stylish.

Right: Natural unstained rattan matchstick shades with warm beige accent threads add a casual elegance to the dining area.

Below: Ring topped valance over woven wood shade.

Custom rendering by DreamDraper® design software, www.dreamdraper.com © 2009 Evan Marsh Designs, Inc.

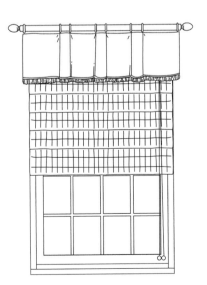

Above: Black-out cordless shades are great in children's rooms — no cords means greater safety and black-out means...they'll sleep longer? One can only hope.

Left: Sophisticated chocolate brown shades are neat and modern.

Below: Pleated shade with arched pleated shade at top.

Multiple sets of cellular shades can be installed on a single headrail. Notice how well the shade blocks the sun, as well as the absence of lift cords and mechanisms. This is a cordless single cell honeycomb, light and sturdy with exceptional privacy and light blocking capabilities.

Left: This designer solar shade is a great choice for above a sink area where privacy isn't a huge issue — but sun control is. *Right*: Bright white opacity is knockdown beautiful in this clean, modern bathroom. It was a good choice to afix the shade slightly lower to allow sun in and emphasize the window architecture.

Left:This classy shade keeps the busy world at bay when completely lowered, offering a modern, textured appearance. Plus, its updated clutch system allows for easy lifting and precise positioning. *Right*: The sunscreen fabric used in these flat panel Roman shades softens the room by maintaining an outdoor view while blocking harsh sunlight.

Tabbed roller shades let a hint of light through.

Note how these shades offer privacy, and still let the outdoors in.

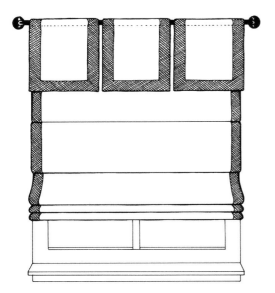

Left: A flat, simple Roman shade draws up into graceful folds. Rod pocket flags decorate the front for added interest.
Right: With a unique tab top and contrast trim, this shade delights.

Above: Fabric/vane combinations such as these Illusions shadings offer diffused light and UV protection along with see through capabilities when open. Rotating the vanes to close position offers exceptional privacy; pulling the shade completely up will stack the vanes and fabric into the headrail.

The Window Decorating Book

Upper left: Treating large window walls is a breeze with fabric/vane verticals.

Middle left: This tailored treatment is a terrific choice in areas where space is at a minimum.
Design by Suzanne Price, Interiors by Decorating Den

Lower left: Silhouette® horizontal fabric/vane treatments, which suspend fabric vanes between two sheer fabric facings, can span a good amount of space without any problem.

Below: Fabric/vane verticals such as Luminette® so closely resemble sheer draperies, one may need to touch them to recognize the difference.

(*Left*) Honeycomb shades are one of today's most versatile and fashionable window coverings. With unique cellular construction and superior sound absorption, selections can range from light filtering to room darkening. Consider a vertical application, too, for sliding glass doors, closet doors or even as room dividers.

(*Right*) Pleated shades are light and airy and are capable of conforming to many different applications, from small to large to odd shapes as well. Note the great width they are able to span, due to solid but lightweight construction.

(*Left*) Flat Roman shades with cord lock and blackout lining hang flat when lowered and fold up neatly when fully raised.

(*Right*) Honeycomb arch shades are energy efficient and are available in many attractive colors.

Above: Cheery red ballon shades enhanced with tassel fringe offer an exhilerating pop of enchanting color. Red is the color of passion and excitement, but when paired with the feminity of billowing fabric, it becomes more about flirting than seduction. Design by Linda Granville & Linda Edwards, Interiors by Decorating Den.

Left: As full and pretty as a petticoat, this London shade is striking but not overpowering, allowing the beautiful casegoods to partner in its success.

Next page: The tone-on-tone stripe makes an elegant statement, drawing out the subtle tones that circle this sophisticated dining area and creating a soothing environment for small talk over a glass of wine.

Above: Flat fold Roman shades provide a buffer from the out of doors with stylish beauty.

Above: Coordinating the fabric shade materials with the wallcovering and upholstered goods is a gamble, but this particular application works tremendously well. Note the pretty green trim lining the bottom of the shade — a nice detail.

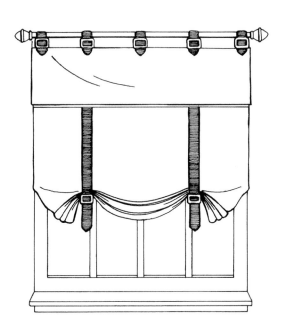

Above left: Flat Roman shade held in place with leather straps with matching buckle tab tops.

Above right: The tabbed hem made of contrast banding on this roller shade is a lovely focal point, also serving the purpose of allowing handling of the shade without damaging or soiling its pretty fabric.

Striped Roman shade is eyecatching.

Ring top flat Roman shade hung on bamboo pole.

Left: Balloon shade with extra pleating and rosettes

Right: London shade with grommets
under scalloped gathered
valance.

Roller shade with decorative edging.

An unlined roll up fabric shade diffuses the bedroom light softly.

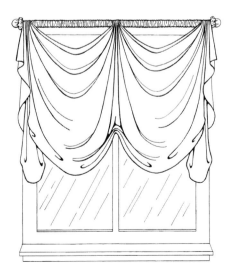

Left: Soft swag-style shade with shirred fabric-covered rod.

Right: Stagecoach shade with contrast straps.

Shades

Design by Sarah Barnard, Sarah Barnard Design

Good to Know

Adding the beauty of fabric into (typically) a smaller space, the fabric shade is a soft touch at the window, perfect for those rooms where fabric is a must, but draperies may be too much.

Of course, this does not mean that fabric shades can't be used in tandem with draperies or curtains — that simply isn't so. You will find soft shades were often used in Victorian interiors, to Art Deco, to today's most fashionable. And you will find soft shades in just about every style — from the very tailored look of a flat Roman shade to the all out utter femininity of a cloud shade, such as the one you see above. Add beads, fringe or other passementerie, even bows or ruffles should you choose to make your shade a bit over the top.

One important aspect to keep in mind, of course, is the lift mechanism and how you will access the cord, be it on the left or right side. Soft shades can also be mechanized, on the off chance that the

mechanism is hard to reach (this might be in the case of a window being behind a piece of furniture, for example).

The most popular styles of soft shades are: the Austrian, which is known for its lovely vertical shirring; the Roman — probably the most popular of them all as it can be quite tailored to lush and drapey; the Balloon/Cloud, both of which are softer looking with plenty of folds; and finally, the roller shade, which you will also see in a "hard" style but can also be made of fabric. This shade will draw up from the bottom and into a tight roll. Of course, there are variations on the shades: the London and the Empire; both of which have similarities to the Cloud/Balloon as well as a host of modifications to the Roman shade.

Shades can also be "hard" — such as made of woven wood, vinyl or other flexible material, but for the purposes of this section, we'll be sticking to fabric.

Inside or Recessed Mounts

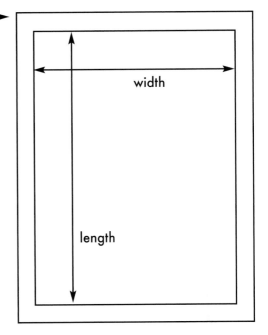

Width

Measure width of window at the top, center and bottom of window. Use the narrowest measurement when ordering. Specify on order form if outside clearance has been made. If no clearance has been allowed, the factory will deduct .25" from the overall width.

Length

Measure the height of the window from top of opening to top of sill, no allowance is made for length.

Outside or Wall Mount

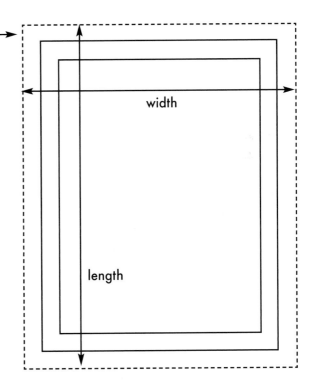

Width

Measure exact width of the area to be covered. It is recommended that shades extend past actual window opening by two inches on each side. Furnish finished shade width, no allowances will be made.

Length

Measure length of area to be covered, allowing a minimum of 2.25" at top of window to accommodate headerboard and brackets. At this time you may want to take into consideration stackage of shades and allow for this in your length measurement. Furnish finished shade length, no allowance will be made.

All Installations

- Specify right or left cord position. If no cord position is indicated, cords will be corded to right hand side.
- Specify cord length (length of cord needed for easy reach, when shade is completely down). If no specification is made, cord will be approximately one-third the length of the shade.
- For pole cloud, cloud and balloon shades, specify if length given is high or low point of pouf.

Fabric Shade Square Footage Chart

Shade Width (in inches)

Shade Length (in inches)	24	30	36	42	48	54	60	66	72	78	84	90	96	102	108	114	120	126	132	138	144
30	10	10	10	10	10	11¼	12½	13¾	15	16¼	17½	18¾	20	21¼	22½	23¾	25	26¼	27½	28¾	30
36	10	10	10	10½	12	13½	15	16½	18	19½	21	22½	24	25½	27	28½	30	31½	33	34½	36
42	10	10	10½	12¼	14	15¾	17½	19¼	21	22¾	24½	26¼	28	29¾	31½	33¼	35	36¾	38½	40¼	42
48	10	10	12	14	16	18	20	22	24	26	28	30	32	34	36	38	40	42	44	46	48
54	10	11¼	13½	15¾	18	20¼	22½	24¾	27	29¼	31½	33¾	36	38¼	40½	42¾	45	47¼	49½	51¾	54
60	10	12½	15	17½	20	22½	25	27½	30	32½	35	37½	40	42½	45	47½	50	52½	55	57½	60
66	11	13¾	16½	19¼	22	24¾	27½	30.¼	33	35¾	38½	41¼	44	46¾	49½	52¼	55	57¾	60½	63¼	66
72	12	15	18	21	24	27	30	33	36	39	42	45	48	51	54	57	60	63	66	69	72
78	13	16¼	19½	22¾	26	29¼	32½	35¾	39	42¼	45½	48¾	52	55¼	58½	61¾	65	68¼	71½	74¾	78
84	14	17½	21	24½	28	31½	35	38½	42	45½	49	52½	56	59½	63	66½	70	73½	77	80½	84
90	15	18¾	22½	26¼	30	33¾	37½	41¼	45	48¾	52½	56¼	60	63¾	67½	71¼	75	78¾	82½	86¼	90
96	16	20	24	28	32	36	40	44	48	52	56	60	64	68	72	76	80	84	88	92	96
102	17	21¼	25½	29¾	34	38¼	42½	46¾	51	55¼	59½	63¾	68	72¼	76½	80¾	85	89¼	93½	97¾	102
108	18	22½	27	31½	36	40½	45	49½	54	58½	63	67½	72	76½	81	85½	90	94½	99	103½	108
114	19	23¾	28½	33¼	38	42¾	47½	52¼	57	61¾	66½	71¼	76	80¾	85½	90¼	95	99¾	104½	109¼	114
120	20	25	30	35	40	45	50	55	60	65	70	75	80	85	90	95	100	105	110	115	120
126	21	26¼	31½	36¾	42	47¼	52½	57¾	63	68¼	73½	78¾	84	89¼	94½	99¾	105	110¼	115½	120¾	126
132	22	27½	33	38½	44	49.5	55	60.5	66	71½	77	82.5	88	93.5	99	104½	110	115½	121	126½	132
138	23	28¼	34½	40¼	46	51¾	47½	63¼	69	74¾	80½	86¼	92	97¾	103½	109¼	115	120¾	126½	132¼	138
144	24	30	36	42	48	54	60	66	72	78	84	90	96	102	108	114	120	126	132	138	144

Cloud Shades

Photo: Arched cloud shade; *illustrations:* Cloud shade variations.

Design by Sarah Barnard, Sarah Barnard Design

This is a fully functional shade with a gathered heading that falls into soft cloud-like poufs. It can be finished with or without a "skirt."

For additional treatments and embellishments, see Appendices beginning on page 288.

Yardage

Step 1 – Width of shade + RT (returns) x 2.5 ÷ width of fabric = number of fabric widths required (round up to whole number)

Step 2a – Shade length + 12" for HH (heading and hems) x widths required ÷ 36 = yardage without pattern repeat (*or*)

Step 2b – Shade length + 12" for HH ÷ pattern repeat = number of repeats required (round up whole number)

Step 2c – Number of repeats x pattern repeat = CL (cut length)

Step 2d – Number of widths x CL ÷ 36 = yardage with pattern repeat (round up to whole number)

Things to Consider

> Color of lining

> Skirt or no skirt

> Left or right pull

Special Notes

1. See page 102 for detailed calculating terms

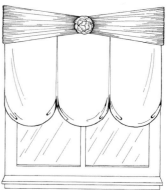

Photo: Balloon shade with trim; *illustrations:* Balloon shade; Balloon shade with hourglass valance

This fully functional shade has large, inverted pleats for a more tailored look. While still billowy looking like the cloud shade, it has a less feminine appearance.

For additional treatments and embellishments, see Appendices beginning on page 288.

Yardage

Step 1 – Width of shade + RT (returns) x 2.5 ÷ width of fabric = number of fabric widths required (round up to whole number)

Step 2a – Shade length + 16" for HH (heading and hems) x widths required ÷ 36 = yardage without pattern repeat (*or*)

Step 2b – Shade length + 12" for HH ÷ pattern repeat = number of repeats required (round up whole number)

Step 2c – Number of repeats required x pattern repeat = CL (cut length)

Step 2d – Number of widths x CL ÷ 36 = yardage with pattern repeat (round up to whole number)

Things to Consider

> Color of lining
> Skirt or no skirt
> Left or right pull

Special Notes

1. See page 102 for detailed calculating terms

Photo: Flat Roman shade; *illustrations:* Flat Roman with decorative edging and tab top; Flat Roman with banding and over-valance.

Design by Sarah Barnard, Sarah Barnard Design

This versatile shade hangs straight but collapses into folds when raised. Fitting many different decors, from casual to traditional to contemporary, and even formal, you can add interest with contrast banding, scalloped edges or pleats.

For additional treatments and embellishments, see Appendices beginning on page 288.

Yardage

Step 1 – Width of shade + 5" ÷ width of fabric = number of fabric widths required (round up to whole number)

Step 2a – Shade length + 10" for HH (heading and hems) x widths required ÷ 36 = yardage without pattern repeat (*or*)

Step 2b – Shade length + 10" for HH ÷ pattern repeat = number of repeats required (round up whole number)

Step 2c – Number of repeats required x pattern repeat = CL (cut length)

Step 2d – Number of widths x CL ÷ 36 = yardage with pattern repeat (round up to whole number)

Things to Consider

> Color of lining
> Right or left pull

Special Notes

1. Not recommended to be wider or longer than 84".
2. Cannot be made with returns.
3. See page 102 for detailed calculating terms.

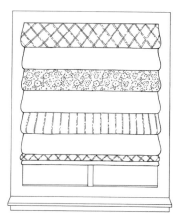

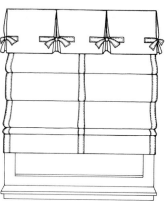

Photo: Folded Roman shade; *illustrations:* Folded Roman with alternating materials; folded Roman with contrast stripes topped with inverted pleat valance.

The folded Roman shade is characterized by its overlapping folds cascading down the full length of the shade.

For additional treatments and embellishments, see Appendices beginning on page 288.

Yardage

Step 1 – Width of shade + 5" ÷ width of fabric = number of fabric widths required (round up to whole number)

Step 2a – Shade length + 10" for HH (heading and hems) x 2 for overlapping folds x widths required ÷ 36 = yardage without pattern repeat (*or*)

Step 2b – Shade length + 10" for HH x 2 ÷ pattern repeat = number of repeats required (round up whole number)

Step 2c – Number of repeats required x pattern repeat = CL (cut length)

Step 2d – Number of widths x CL ÷ 36 = yardage with pattern repeat (round up to whole number)

Things to Consider

> Color of lining
> Right or left pull

Special Notes

1. Folded Roman shades larger than 60" in width or 84" in length are not recommended.

2. Due to the nature of the fabric construction, the folds do not hang evenly; therefore, they are not recommended for an application where two or more are hung side by side.

3. Cannot be made with returns.

4. See page 102 for detailed calculating terms.

Austrian Shade

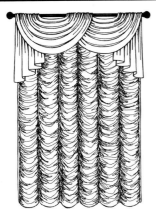

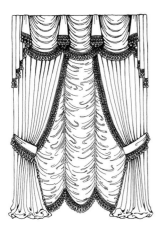

Photo & illustrations: Austrian shades

A soft, formal treatment created by vertical shirring between scallops.

For additional treatments and embellishments, see Appendices beginning on page 288.

Yardage

Step 1 – Width of shade x 1.5 ÷ width of fabric = number of fabric widths required (round up to whole number)

Step 2a – Number of widths x shade length + 10" for HH (heading and hems) x 3 ÷ 36 = yardage without pattern repeat (*or*)

Step 2b – Number of widths x shade length + 10" for HH x 3 ÷ pattern repeat = number of repeats required (round up whole number)

Step 2c – Number of repeats required x pattern repeat = CL (cut length)

Step 2d – Number of widths x CL ÷ 36 = yardage with pattern repeat (round up to whole number)

Things to Consider

> Color of lining (if applicable)
> Right or left cord pull

Special Notes

1. This treatment has a tendency to pull in on the sides. Make sure this will not be a problem.
2. Use heavier fabric for privacy or sheer/lace fabric for a lighter more decorative appearance.
3. Austrians can be used as a single treatment or in combination with draperies or valances.
4. See page 102 for detailed calculating terms

Shades

171

Combinations

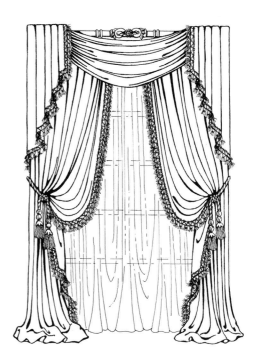

Who says you can't have the best of both worlds? *When* one window treatment isn't enough, the beauty and flexibility of a combination treatment is the perfect way to proceed. Typically, a hard window treatment (such as a blind or shade) is combined with stationary drapery panels...or motorized panels...or a top treatment...or whatever your heart desires. Indeed, it is sometimes the hard treatment that stays, with the soft treatment changing as often as the homeowner wishes.

Left: Floor to ceiling wood blinds and drapery panels make a bold statement. Note how long the lift/tilt cords are for the upper section of blinds. One could also consider motorization as a way to manipulate the blinds in a far easier manner. Nonetheless, this is a gutsy treatment that commands attention — and deserves it. Design by Nancy Barrett, Interiors by Decorating Den

Above: Sheer underdraperies; puddled panels; decorative hardware; swags, bullion fringe — this treatment has it all!

173

History in the Making

By the 17th century, window treatments were a distinct and planned element in the design of an interior. Layer upon layer of fabric, created specifically for draping, unveiled complex and ornate works of window art. Coupled with flat woven braids, fringe, opulent tassels and darling rosettes, combination treatments were lush beauties to behold with their rich colors in gold, red and blue, vibrant tapestries, and heavy silks and cottons.

By the mid-18th century, combination treatments had begun to evolve into something more easily equated with today's interiors. Roller blinds crafted of natural linen, rather than heavy undertreatments, were in charge of sun control, for example. Shutters, another favorite, were coupled with pretty curtains.

Left: Note how the use of both horizontal and vertical fabric/vane shades add interest to this tall window wall, with a stationary drapery panel to bridge the change.

Above: Pole mounted swags are enhanced with decorative hardware and trim.

Today's Combinations

Today, combinations come in many configurations, but at their best, they couple to fulfill the needs of today's consumer: a hard "under" treatment, such as a blind or shade takes care of the elements of privacy and sun control. A fabric "over" treatment softens the window, adds a splash of color and provides focus and impetus to the design of the room. Finally, a top treatment, such as a cornice or valance, finishes the top and conceals any architectural flaws or unsightly drapery hardware.

Below: Board mounted swag and tail treatments couple with fabric/vane verticals in this luxe sitting area. The use of color in this room is particularly stunning with its pinks, oranges and aquas, coupled with the more sedate neutral beiges. While muted, the colors are also lively and inviting.

Right: Sheer underdraperies are flanked with bullion trimmed side panels and a swag and jabot top treatment with decorative trimmings.

The Facts: Combinations

Advantages: Offers the functional nature of a hard treatment, coupled with the beauty of fabric; in future years, you could, for example, leave the hard treatment and have a new overtreatment installed, thus changing the entire look of the room without the expense of an entirely new treatment

Disadvantages: Cost: more layers equal more money; needs (typically) a larger space to accommodate the multiple layers; treatments may not wear at the same rate.

Cost: These treatments are some of the most expensive being there are so many layers, including a hard treatment such as wood blinds, shutters or cellular shades, coupled with a sheer undertreatment, a fabric overtreatment (or two), and even a cornice to complete the look. Count on your costs reaching into the thousands of dollars.

Lifespan: Varying, depending upon the types of treatments being used. Remember that fabric has a lower life expectancy than hard treatments such as blinds. You may find that you have to replace one layer, while the other is still perfectly fine.

Most Appropriate Locations: Anywhere that there is space that will accommodate both hard and soft choices. Typically seen most often in dining and living rooms, period-style homes, elaborate sitting rooms and bedrooms.

Care & Cleaning: Each treatment may require a different type of care. Refer to specific chapters within this book for more specialized information.

Left: Crisp pleated shades offer lift systems that raise a window treatment with ease and precision. The addition of stationary drapery panels offer an interesting vertical element to the horizontal nature of the shades. Note, too, that this is a light filtering shade — an added neutral backing would help to provide privacy if needed.

Above: Lush rod pocket contrast lined draperies anchored with rosette tiebacks couple with matching shade and fabric/vane undertreatment — a matchless combination.

Below: Made from select natural woods, including reeds, bamboo and grasses, these woven wood shades are uniquely textured, adding casual good looks. The draperies soften and pull together the unusual wall color patterns.

Combinations

On this sweeping window wall, trillion-shaped chocolate brown upholstered cornices encase lengthy drapery panels. Pleated shades installed in the lower bank offer privacy when needed. Design by Barbara Elliot & Jennifer Ward Woods, Interiors by Decorating Den

This unusual dropped ceiling is a tough act to follow, especially with the inset orange neon lighting. But this combination treatment is the perfect solution. Long casual scarves drape through scarf brackets mounted just below the drop with wood blinds to offer privacy and light control when need be. Leaving the window architecture untreated was a good choice as it is beautiful in its own right.

Enjoy a few more lush styles (below).
Trillian cornices are the foundation for three beautiful window treatments, all with swag accents.
All three illustrations below thanks to Patterns Plus Design, www.patternsplus.com.

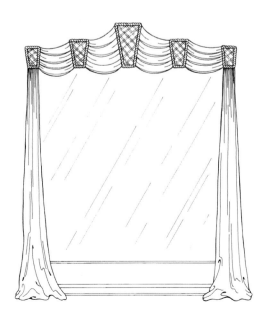

Good to Know: Combinations

- If you will be manipulating the hard treatment regularly, it may not be necessary to have an operational soft treatment. Consider stationary panels flanking your window for a softened look.

- Make certain your hard treatment offers the privacy and sun control measures you desire; otherwise, your soft treatment should be operational in order accommodate your priorities.

- Consider a top treatment to cover the multiple pieces of window hardware needed to hang your other window treatments.

- To change the look of your draperies seasonally, consider a removable drapery swag, which typically attaches to the front of a stationary panel, hooking to the same rings as the stationary treatment. Perhaps in winter, a lushly fringed velvet swag in a deep cognac tone will add holiday cheer to a patterned drapery panel, while in summer, a small string of silk flowers or an unlined blue silk swag will coordinate and lighten the look.

- Know that while your initial expense may be higher for a combination treatment, subsequent redressings of the window may only require a change of fabric, while the hard treatment stays.

Above left: Traversing draperies layer over a soft cornice — a beautiful combination. Design by Bonnie Pressley, Interiors by Decorating Den

Above right: Classic pole swag offset by pleated drapery panels and flip top bellpull-style treatments.

Long bellpull-style panels stretch from ceiling height in dramatic fashion with scalloped roller shades as a partner.

Design by Theresa Zadravec, Interiors by Decorating Den

Combinations

Above: Low level furniture grounds this room; the ceiling high drapery panels with accompanying blinds do much to draw the eye up.

Design by Lynne Lawson, Interiors by Decorating Den

The Window Decorating Book

Upper left: The pinstripe pattern of these natural wood fiber woven shades, combined with simple drapery panels, creates a tailored layered look.

Middle left: Decorative rods hold luxe drapery panels and provide accent to the hard horizontal blind treatment. Design by Diana Apgar, Interiors by Decorating Den

Lower left: A pretty box pleat valance provides crisp detail to the hard treatment and dramatic striped drapery panels.

Below: What could be prettier than sunny yellow in the morning when you wake up? This three layer treatment has it all, with cornice, sheers and a fabric/vane combination for privacy and sun control.

Upper right: One of the great debates in the window treatment arena is whether or not to cover architectural details. Of course, when the architecture is flawed, it must be covered, but when it is as lovely as a ceiling height arch, the treatment must be completed with tact and imagination. In this application, the architecture remains a focal point, done to perfection, with beautiful hardware, expertly crafted arch top, a sophisticated color palette and fabric/vane shades to complete.
Design by Sharon Binkerd, Interiors by Decorating Den

Upper left: Simple rod pocket drapery panels combine with inside mount shades. A sleek, modern combination for smaller spaces.

Lower right: Layers of fabric make this master bedroom area an opulent retreat. In this application the balloon valance is inoperable, as are the drapery panels. All privacy for this room is provided by the fabric/vane shades. The dark chocolate brown drapery folds are truly sophisticated. This is a combination that succeeds on all levels.
Design by Sharon Binkerd, Interiors by Decorating Den

Lower left: Lush side panels lined with contrast fabric are well protected from the sun when used in conjunction with a fabric/vane combination, which can filter the light or block it completely, depending upon your needs. The draperies are not so fussy, either, that they couldn't be released from their tiebacks and be allowed to drape across the window.

Design by Courtney Willard, Interiors by Decorating Den

Above: The timeless appeal of ring top panels are enhanced with the addition of natural woven Roman shades fitting cleanly between the vertical frames of the windows. The neutral, golden tone of the shades ties the room's furnishings and woodwork together with the window — a stunning combination.

Left: Tailored soft cornices above the hard edges of the shutter fit nicely into this corner area, softening without taking up a lot of space.

Below: Board mounted designer-style soft cornice with tail over puddled stationary drapery panel. Custom rendering by DreamDraper® design software, www.dreamdraper.com © 2009 Evan Marsh Designs, Inc.

Above: Nailhead cornices hold striped drapery panels and lovely scalloped soft cornices. Note, too, the fabric covered ceiling. This is a room that implies a sense of decadence, of East Indian opulence.

Right: Peach draperies swag elegantly with opulent puddling onto the terra cotta tiles below. An interesting use of light fringe masks mounting hardware. Notice, too, behind the drapery panel lies a translucent sheer to pull across the window opening when the sun is at its most fierce.

Below: Asymmetrical goblet pleated drapery enhanced with tiny cascade, tassels and braiding.

Combinations

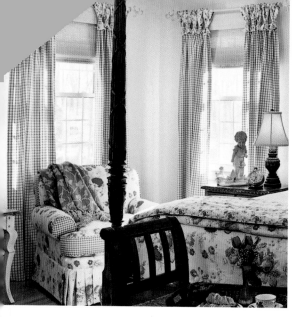

Above left: Gingham checks coupled with patterned fabric on decorative rods are a lovely accompaniment to solid color shades. Design by D. J. Smith, Interiors by Decorating Den

Middle Left: Classic panel shutters with 3½" louvers provide the privacy and light control; stationary fabric side panels hung from decorative iron scarf holders add the softness. Note how easy it would be to change out the fabric portion of this combination while leaving the shutters in place. This is a terrific example of how a combination treatment can be less expensive to redo on subsequent redecoration.

Lower Left: This is a treatment with a lot going on, but to perfection. Pristine drapery panels with shirred tiebacks are attached underneath a curved, upholstered cornice. It's a lovely treatment made even more elegant with the addition of a blush pink swag, tail and rosette top treatment, which pulls in coloration from the decorative ceiling.

Below: A large-scale print fabric shade complements the plain silk panels.

A scalloped, box-pleated valance in explosive orange/red, enhanced with decorative trim, accompanies dramatic side panels.

Combinations

Chocolate brown ring and rod drapery panels enhance creamy pleated shades.

Top left: A pretty soft cornice, constructed swag-style, is a great treatment for this guest room. With a small area, the treatment softens the room without overpowering it. Pleated shades finish the space, to provide privacy in the evening.

Bottom left: A highly detailed wood cornice holds elegantly trimmed drapery panels, beautifully simple and elegant.

Top right: Rod pocket sheers play gracefully with the floor and pop against the blue walls. The shade undertreatment coordinates with the bedspread and pillow accents.

Bottom right: Designer tab top panels flank a scalloped roller shade trimmed in fringe.

Combinations

Top Treatments

When your heart says "beautiful window covering," but your room says "not enough space!" the solution is a stunning top treatment. From a soft swag dipping gracefully across a window to the hard edges of a wood cornice, the function of a top treatment is to provide beauty to a home, hide the mechanics of an additional window treatment, disguise architectural flaws and also to emphasize and draw focus to a window. By itself or as a beautiful punctuation, valances, cornices and swags (the lion's share of the top treatment category) are excellent choices when dressing a window.

Left: This classic pole swag exhibits all of the fine characteristics of the venerable top treatment. The assymetrical shorter tail is a perfect means to keep the treatment from becoming overly heavy (imagine if the swag had hosted longer panels on both sides — the treatment would have overpowered this smaller window). The brush fringe is a terrific choice for decorative trimming and the petite polka dot adds interest. An exceptionally well-done window covering. Design by Ruth Zerbe, Interiors by Decorating Den

Above: Layered swags with puddled panels are shabby chic.

History in the Making

The earliest recorded history of interior design is rooted in the Renaissance Era, a time of great change and rebirth in the world of art and architecture. Much of this era saw understated, simple treatments, moving toward more elaborate bed coverings and portieres (fabric panels for doors), and onto multiple layered treatments, including, toward the end of this period, valances, swags and pelmets. By the Baroque and Early Georgian period (1643–1730), elaborate and theatrical treatments placed high emphasis on the cornice and pelmet as a way to finish off the top of a window treatment.

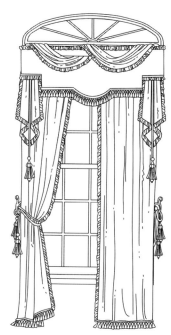

Left: It is the upholstered cornice that ties this bedroom together with its harlequin pattern — such an ideal complement to the checked and toile fabric used in the bedding and drapery panel. The scalloped lower edge displays stylish beading, popping nicely against the white of the hard treatment. Note also that the cornice hides all of the hardware and mechanisms associated with the hard treatment and the toile drapery panel.
Design by Barbara Elliot & Jennifer Ward Woods, Interiors by Decorating Den

Above: Elaborately trimmed cornice with swags and tails cap trimmed drapery panels with tassel tiebacks.
Custom rendering by DreamDraper® design software, www.dreamdraper.com
© 2009 Evan Marsh Designs, Inc.

Today's Top Treatments

Today, the choices are many for top treatments. In fact, it is frequently noted that the top treatment allows much more creative exploration for the designer and workroom due to its smaller scale. "Theme" cornices are often a favorite in children's rooms: baseball pennants at the top of a cornice or ballet slippers used as a decorative element to secure the corners of a small swag. A single handkerchief swag will punctuate a bathroom window; and elaborate padded and upholstered cornice will add beautiful emphasis to sumptuous draperies.

Below: Green silk scarves swag gently over decorative poles to soften the window area without impeding the view. It is their simplicity that is so appealing. While there is certainly room for drapery panels — or multi-layered treatments for that matter — the lack of fuss at the window is very pleasing to the eye.

Right: Scarf swag hangs asymmetrically for maximum impact. Custom rendering by DreamDraper® design software, www.dreamdraper.com
© 2009 Evan Marsh Designs, Inc.

The Facts: Top Treatments

Advantages: Perfect for areas that may not be able to accommodate a full curtain or drapery, such as above a kitchen sink or in other areas where floor space may be limited or blocked; can hide architectural flaws, such as windows placed at different heights; can quickly soften a hard treatment; can introduce a beautiful focal point to any room

Disadvantages: Not particularly useful for issues of privacy or sun control; can gather dust due to the stationary nature of the treatment; can overpower a small window if not designed properly

Cost: Can vary depending upon the type of top treatment. For example, a solid wood or wrought iron cornice may be quite a bit more costly than a chipboard cornice, padded and covered with fabric; a swag and tail treatment is usually more costly than a scarf.

Lifespan: Years+

Most Appropriate Locations: Anywhere that a window needs softening but space is at a premium. As always, do keep fabric away from areas of extreme moisture to cut back on issues of mold growth and/or fabric discoloration.

Care & Cleaning: Depending upon the type of treatment, you may be able to vacuum or dust at the window, or remove and dust, or remove and have cleaned professionally. Do not attempt to wash your top treatments conventionally.

Left: In a sunny kitchen, privacy is accomplished with short café curtains. The pretty blue and green valance, however, melds the room. Note how detailed the green band is with its multiple pleats and how the chair tops have a matching slip cover to coordinate.

Above: Scalloped soft cornices with tassel accent hide the hard shade treatments. Design by Beverly Barrett, Interiors by Decorating Den

Below: Attached directly to each of the French doors, the upholstered treatments do not impede egress but do provide beautiful accent. Note that the pattern is also picked up in the chair cushions and wallcovering. A nice touch was choosing yellow walls for the dining area rather than more of the wallcovering, which would have overpowered the space. Design by Beverly Barrett, Interiors by Decorating Den

The Window Decorating Book

Left: This unusual top treatment is a marriage of valance and swag with pretty contrast lining peeping out from underneath the deep folds. While the treatment is hung from rings, this is definitely a stationary window covering.

Design by Connie Thompson, Interiors by Decorating Den

Above: A green striped cornice finishes off the top of this window in style, housing the hardware that holds the matching pinch pleat draperies. This mossy green blends well with the walls and accent pieces, creating a soothing blend.

Good to Know: Top of the Line

What's the difference between a cornice and a lambrequin? A valance and a pelmet? Here's a look:

Balloon: A soft fabric valance that is billowy and lush, drooping in graceful, looping folds across the top of a window. Also known as a cloud, though the shape varies slightly.

Box pleat: A flat, symmetrical fold of cloth sewn in place to create fullness, spaced evenly across the top of a drapery. The fabric can be folded back on either side of the pleat to show, for example, a contrasting fabric.

Cascade: A zig-zag shaped piece of fabric falling gracefully from the top of a drapery or top treatment. Can also be called as an ascot or jabot, depending upon the shape and pleat pattern used.

Cornice: A rigid treatment that sometimes serves as a mask for holding attached stationary draperies or for hiding various window treatment hardware or even masking architectural flaws. The cornice is typically constructed of a chipboard-style wood or lightweight material over which some kind of padding is placed, then covered with a fabric of choice and finished with decorative trim or cording to cover any seams. Only fits across the top of a window frame. Can be a terrific focal point; usually mounted on the outside of a window frame.

Jabot: A stationary panel, decorative in nature, used in tandem with a swag (festoon). Also known as a tail.

Lambrequin: An extended version of the cornice, the lambrequin not only fits across the top of the window frame but also extends down on either side, resembling legs. Shaped or straight, this three-sided piece is created in much the same manner as a cornice, but is typically more elaborately decorated. Also called a cantonniere.

Pelmet: Much like a valance, only the fabric has been stiffened and shaped and then embellished with a variety of decorative edgings, including trims, tassels or color bands.

Rosette: Fabric gathered into the shape of a flower. Typically placed at the top right and left corners of a window frame to accent an existing treatment, such as a scarf or drapery panel.

A pretty cloud valance is graceful with its billowing folds in this luxurious sunroom. Long wood beads alternating in black and white are an elegant contrast. Note that the treatment has been ruched onto a mock cornice of about four to five inches in width — an easy way to hang such an elaborate treatment.
Design by Rebecca Shearn, Interiors by Decorating Den

Above: Three layers of fabric: sheers, silk panels and a stationary tied-back drapery panel are enhanced by a fourth and fifth layer: a luscious seven fold board-mounted swag with accompanying tail top treatment. Notice, too, how the treatment also works beautifully as a corona over the bed frame — a sweeping focal point.

Scarf: A single, lengthy piece of lightweight fabric with a color/pattern that shows on both sides (as opposed to simply being imprinted on one side) that either wraps loosely around a stationary rod, or loops through decorative brackets placed on either side of a window frame.

Swag & Tail: A section of draped fabric at the top of the window that typically resembles a sideways "C" shape (swag) sometimes coupled with a vertical "tail" which hangs on either side of the swag. There are many kinds of swag top treatments, but the prevalent styles are the basic pole swag or the bias swag, which can either be hung in a variety of ways, including from a cornice box, a pole or attached directly to the inside of a window frame.

Valance: A simple to elaborate treatment, the valance is a piece of decorative fabric usually hung from a rod, a piece of decorative hardware or a board. Valances can take on many shapes: poufed, scalloped, pointed, arched, and rectangular and can also be pleated or gathered.

Left: Striped fabrics are some of the hardest to swag, but this tassel trimmed pole mounted swag and tails is perfectly executed.

Below: A bay window has been treated to the formal beauty of ring mounted swags over stationary drapery panels. Note that the treatment works well in the (*right*) double hung window, too.

Design by J. White, Interiors by Decorating Den

Awning

Balloon Valance

Butterfly Valance

Cornice-Soft

Cornice-Upholstered

Cornice-Wood

Top Treatments

Some of the more common top treatment styles include:

This page:

Upper row, left: An awning valance is a quaint take on the more large, commercial-style awning.

Upper row, middle: A balloon valance is known for its billowing folds of fabric.

Upper row, right: A butterfly valance is drawn up on either end so that the form is similar to a butterfly's shape. Can be drawn up with straps or shirred.

Middle row, left: A soft cornice is known for its soft bottom and rigid top.

Middle row, middle: An upholstered cornice is padding and fabric over a chipboard frame.

Middle row, right: Wood cornices are rigid and often have other window treatment components installed inside of them.

Next page:

Upper row, left: A gathered valance is really just fabric shirred over a large, flat rod, typically about four inches in diameter.

Upper row, middle: A jabot is a piece of decorative fabric used in conjunction with a swag.

Upper row, right: A kingston valance incorporates the jabot into the swag.

Middle row, left: A box pleated valance shows flat, symmetrical folds across the face of the valance.

Middle row, middle: A rod pocket valance is created with a pocket through which a rod is fed.

Middle row, right: A scarf is a single piece of fabric that wraps loosely around a rod or bracket.

Lower row, left: A board mounted swag is stapled to a board to hold its shape in place.

Lower row, middle: A pole swag drapes gracefully over a rod.

Lower row, right: A tab/tie valance is tied or has a rod fed through its built-in loops.

Gathered Valance

Jabot

Kingston Valance

Pleated (Box) Valance

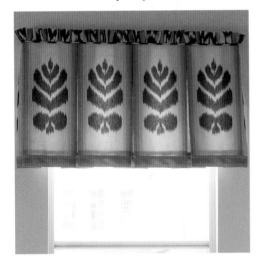

Rod Pocket Valance

Scarf

Swag-Board Mounted

Swag-Pole Mounted

Tab/Tie Valance

Above: A classic pole-mounted swag and zig zag tail is mounted at the ceiling to provide height to this room and also better access to the swinging windows. The same fabric is used on the sofa pillows, too — a nice touch.

Left: A beautiful wood cornice, intricately carved, emphasizes the bay window and houses the mounting hardware for the classic swag and tail top treatment, as well as the fabric/vane privacy treatment.

Below: Elaborately trimmed swags and jabots enhance stationary drapery panels. Custom rendering by DreamDraper® design software, www.dreamdraper.com © 2009 Evan Marsh Designs, Inc.

Floral fabric on this simple pole swag treatment provides a well-designed pop of vibrancy against the full, green draperies.

Top Treatments

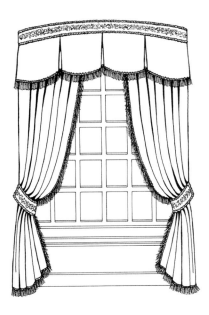

Left: Inverted pleats and a curved hem coupled with dainty candy stripes make this simple valance a true pleaser.

Above left: With tails approximately five inches lower than the center, this valance is well constructed and stylish. Note, too, that the fabric is picked up in accent pillows, a common but delightful design trick.

Below left: An arched box pleated valance edged with brush fringe, paired with pleated, matching drapery panels, are simply elegant.

Above right: An inverted box pleat valance in a wild pink animal print is suitable for any cat. Note the accent pillow in the same fabric and how well it works with large scale floral patterns, too.

Below right: Soft cornice with jabots and rosettes.

Above: Vibrant red pole swags with contrast lining (you can see it in the tail area) are a dramatic accent to the hard shutter undertreatment.

Left: This bias swag and tail top treatment is mounted on the same rings as the stationary drapery panel. Opulent bullion fringe provides nice contrast.

Below: Fan pleated draperies are accented with simple swag and tail accompaniment.

Above: This Scandinavian-style scarf treatment is casual and easy. Also appreciated is the use of complementary fabrics, rather than using the same fabric for both doorways.

Right: Sheer handkerchief swags with long, flowing tails accentuate the tall window wall without detracting from the view outside.

Below: Multiple scarf swag treatments accents the window without overpowering it. Custom rendering by DreamDraper® design software, www.dreamdraper.com © 2009 Evan Marsh Designs, Inc.

The Window Decorating Book

Above left: Beige and white checked cloud shades, trimmed in small tassel fringe, complement stationary drapery panels and are echoed as a valance above the bed with graceful style.

Below left: A classic upholstered cornice fits snugly around the window frame, hiding the mechanisms for the underlying Roman shade.

Below right: A wood cornice adds architectural interest to an otherwise humdrum window frame.

Below: Golden plaid valances echo the many curved and v-shaped motifs in this bedroom, such as the floral print above the bed, the footboard, the headboard and the rounded edge of the accent table.

Right: Beautiful swags accented with rosettes are a powerful statement at the window.

Above: This Moorish cornice coupled with multiple sheer treatments is a
delight. With 18 foot ceilings, this was a treatment that needed to pull out all
of the stops. Taking inspiration from engravings of the Victorian era (there was
a proclivity toward Morrish design in that time period), six and a half foot
wide by seven foot high cornices, covered in iridescent slubby silk, were
designed to anchor the room. Two layers of sheers come down from behind
the cornices.

Left: Peek-a-boo contrast lining swoops below the swag-like edges of this trim
laden decorative cornice,
hiding horizontal blind
hardware and making a
small window ultimately
special.

Adjacent: Bishop sleeve
draperies with thickly
braided ties and arched
cornice follow the
window shape well.
Patterns Plus Design;
www.patttternsplus.com

Above: A simple striped soft cornice conceals the mounting and lift hardware for a classic flatfold Roman shade. Note that the Roman shade to the right of the photograph coordinates with the soft cornice — a really good move on the part of the designer.

Right: A beige upholstered cornice with tone-on-tone welt cord trim is clean and unfussy above a tailored, lined shade.

Below: Soft edged cornice with puddled stationary draperies offer a peek of the window arch above. Custom rendering by DreamDraper® design software, www.dreamdraper.com
© 2009 Evan Marsh Designs, Inc.

A vibrant green upholstered cornice showcases the graceful scarf treatment, hung swag-style over the top and cascading on each side. The green is verdant, working well with accessories and other upholstered goods to pull this room together stylishly.

Design by Theresa Zadravec, Interiors by Decorating Den

A wood cornice painted in eye catching metallic gold is the beautiful apparatus to house the soft drapes of a Kingston valance and accompanying drapery panels. The gold accents pop well against the dark green wallpaper.

Design by Kathy Dyer, Interiors by Decorating Den

Contrast lined swag treatments are a lush treat, dressing the architecturally beautiful windows without pulling complete attention from their own inherent beauty. This lovely treatment draws the focus up and toward the 90 degree windows. Truly a great design choice.
Design by Barbara Elliot & Jennifer Ward Woods, Interiors by Decorating Den

This assymetrical scarf is a true delight, its slightly off-kilter style a playful accent to an otherwise formal billiard room. Notice, too, how just the touch of green passementerie manages to pull together all other elements of the room, from the green of the billiards table to the touches of green in the rug and also the accent pillows on the sofa. Try to imagine this room without the scarf. It wouldn't be quite as nice, would it?

Right: Soft and airy, this cloud valance with decorative trim is a pretty accent to the privacy providing shutters, fitting perfectly within the bay window.

Middle: A classic swag and tail arrangement is naturally beautiful over drapery panels and a sheer undertreatment.

Left: An elaborately swagged board-mounted valance is a graceful accent in this music room. Note the lovely crystal finial midway — an ideal means to provide a flourish of detail.

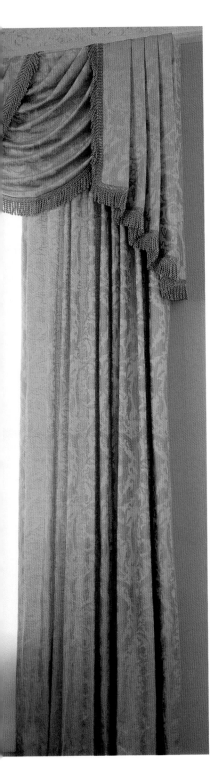

Right: An upholstered cornice and hold-back exhibit stunning workmanship. Design by Barbara Elliott/Jennifer Ward Woods, Interiors by Decorating Den; photo by Jeff Sanders

Middle: Decorative braid trims the edges of the two upholstered cornices. Notice that one cornice rounds a corner, while the other is straight. Design by Angela Palmer, Interiors by Decorating Den; photo by Jeff Sanders

Left: Rounded detailing add a lovely accent and mirror the shape of the swags.

Above: A Kingston valance caps a Roman shade. Design by Susan Owens, Interiors by Decorating Den; photo by Richard Ruthkatz

Left: A simple box-pleated valance is perfect for this small area. Design by Jeanne Sallee, Interiors by Decorating Den; photo by Jeff Sanders

Below: Empire valance with rosettes complements the crisp pleats of the stationary drapery panels.

Above: Flip top soft valance ehxibits contrast fabric. Design by Lynne Lawson, Interiors by Decorating Den; photo by Randy Foulds

Right: A simple upholstered cornice with ripple detailing is enhanced with delicate trim. Design by Diane Apgar, Interiors by Decorating Den; photo by Randy Foulds

Below: Stationary cuffed drapery panels with striped Roman shade.

Top Treatments

224   The Window Decorating Book

Above left: Soft swagged valance hung by metal holdbacks are made of the same fabric as the adjacent swag. Design by Kathy Machir, Interiors by Decorating Den; photo by Zack Benson

Below left: Nautical rope detailing on an upholstered cornice. Design by Jeanne Grier, Interiors by Decorating Den; photo by Johnny Trigiani

Below right: Crisp triangle accent on the soft cornice is the upside down mimic of the sharp, steep ceiling. Design by Barbara Elliott/Jennifer Ward Woods, Interiors by Decorating Den; photo by Jeff Sanders

Below: Swagged valance hides drapery hardware. Design by Joyce Means, Interiors by Decorating Den; photo by Edie Ellison

Right: Empire valance is accented with rosettes; simply pleated draperies with rosette medallions complete the look.

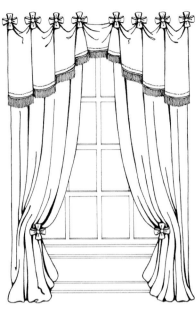

Design by Patty Hughes, Interiors by Decorating Den

Above: A top treatment with a lot of detail, from the graceful curves to the jabot pleats to the detailed rosettes.

Left: Casual fan-style pinch pleats enhance a ring top valance.

Below: A lovely swag and cascade is accented with petite tassels and trim; uncomplicated drapery panels serve as a backdrop.

Above: Flip top stationary draperies cascade over the top of upholstered cornices, accentuated with delicate passementerie. Design by Alisa Lankenau/Heidi Sowatsky, Interiors by Decorating Den; photo by Bob Hill

Right: Gold and white fringe follows the line of the sheer swag, which is held in place with a metal swagholder.

Below: Intricate cornices, lush swags and Bishop sleeved drapery panels make for an unforgettable treatment.

Good to Know

Ever thought about what it might take to create your own swag? Well, following are the basic measurements and specifications you will need to put together a simple swag and cascade treatment.

From the previous pages on top treatments, you have probably discerned that swags are a special kind of top treatment, capable of standing alone or also as an accent to a drapery or blind, among other things. There are many kinds of swag top treatments, but the prevalent styles are the basic pole swag or the bias swag, which can either be hung in a variety of ways, including from a cornice box, a pole or attached directly to the inside of a window frame.

Usually crafted into soft, graceful folds, you should look for a fabric that drapes easily, rather than something stiff and somewhat unyielding. Also, when using swags in multiples, shoot for an odd, rather than even number for better symmetry. Finally, be sure to line your swag, not just for sun protection, but also so that the sun doesn't leak through the fabric unevenly. You see, near the top where the folds are heavier and even somewhat above the window panes, the light will be blocked more so than where the folds drape. This will cause the fabric color to look uneven. By lining your fabric, you create a sturdier swag and one that remains the same color throughout.

Over the next couple of pages, we will look at a variety of swag and cascade treatments, and what you will need to specify to create a wonderful accent in your home. Later on, we'll also cover a few valance styles such as cloud, balloon, box-pleated and also a traditional cornice box. Let's begin.

Swag & Cascade Specifications

For standard room and window sizes, the preferable swag width size is 20" to 40" wide and has a vertical drop (finished length) of 16" to 20". Swags in this range only require 1.5 yards of fabric if lined, or three yards if self-lined (recommended). Swags between 40" and 60" require two yards of fabric if lined, or four yards if self-lined. These yardages are for plain fabrics only. For swags wider than 60" or with patterned fabrics, especially stripes, please consult a professional designer or drapery workroom.

The area to be covered and windows behind the swags are important considerations. Does the area to be covered include one, two or three separate windows? Balancing the swag placement in front of multiple windows is an important design element. If only one large window is to be covered, then swag placement is much easier. (*For detailed yardage requirements: see specific swag type on the following pages.*)

Swag Widths & Board Face

Since swags vary in width and length, the folds will also vary in quantity and size. Very small swags have only a few folds and extremely wide swags will have a limited drop length. You will determine the width of the swags by the Board Face. The board face means the width of the board the swags will be installed upon prior to being mounted across the top to the window.

Traditional (overlapping) Swag Sizes and Quantities

Traditional swags overlap; therefore you will need to add an allowance for overlapping into your calculations. Swag overlaps will start approximately one-half, or less, of the width of the swag face. Swag widths when overlapped = length of board face divided by the number of swags + 8".

For example, let's say your board face is 127" wide and you want five swags: 127 ÷ 5 = 25.4 (round to whole number of 26); 26 + 8 = 34", or the width of each swag face. This allows for 8" overlapping for each swag. Since the final swag width of 34" is between 20" and 40" this would make five swags an excellent choice for an area to be covered of 127". Caution: the 8" overlap rule may need to be adjusted down to 4", 2" or 0" for a small board face with mul-

tiple swags. Example, a 40" board face with three swags would result in reducing the overlap to 2". 40 ÷ 3 = 14. 14 + 2 = 16" swag face widths. That's plenty of overlap.

Linear (non-overlapping) Swag Sizes and Quantities

Linear swags don't overlap; therefore you don't need to add for overlapping allowance. It's easier to figure swag face widths for linear swags because you simply divide the board face by the number of desired swags. Example: A board face of 127 ÷ 5 (desired swags) = 5 swags that are 27" wide. Since 27" is between 20" and 40" that would be appropriate for swag face widths. But since 127 ÷ 4 = 31, that would also be appropriate for swag face widths. Keep in mind that that fewer swags mean less cost. You could also use three swags because 127 ÷ 3 = 42" swag face widths. Jabots or horns are usually required to hide the open spaces left when using linear swags.

Standard Drop Lengths

Since swag length, or drop, is usually one fifth of the drapery length, or a close approximation, the standard drop lengths of swags are 16" for an 84" drapery treatment, and 20" for a 96" long drapery treatment.

Soft swag and jabot cornice over puddled side panels.

Photo: Swags installed under wood cornice box; *illustration:* Swag valance over drapery panels on a French door. Custom rendering by DreamDraper® design software, www.dreamdraper.com © 2009 Evan Marsh Designs, Inc.

There are many varieties of swags, cascades and jabots; unfortunately, many professionals use different terms used to describe the same elements. While in the UK the term "tail" is used to describe a cascade or jabot, in the US some professionals use the term jabot to describe a cascade. Both are correct, it is simply a matter of personal preference. Here we will use the term jabot to describe decorative pieces of fabric (usually smaller than cascades) that are hung over seams or between swags or swag-like valances including Kingston, Empire or Austrian valances, to name a few. Jabots may be tie-shaped, cone-shaped, rounded at the bottom or even look like a small cascade.

A cascade is a folded piece of fabric that falls from the top of a drapery heading, swag or valance to create a sort of zigzag, or cascading effect. Because you will no doubt see the interior of the cascade as it folds back onto itself, cascades must be lined with either contrast lining or self-lined (with its own fabric).

For additional treatments and embellishments, see Appendices beginning on page 288.

Yardage: Cascades

For self-lined cascades double the longest length or point of the cascade then add four inches (for tack, or attaching strip) then divide by 36 to supply you with the proper amount of yardage needed for a single pair of cascades. This calculation is for a cascade width (face) up to 14". For contrast-lined cascades add 4" to the longest point of the cascade and divide by 36.

Photo: Soft cornice with bullion-trimmed jabot; *illustrations:* Various cascade and jabot styles with swags Custom renderings by DreamDraper® design software, www.dreamdraper.com © 2009 Evan Marsh Designs, Inc.

Single or Double, Traditional Cascade Yardage

Please note that the yardages specified below are for a single pair of cascades.

Lined in contrasting fabric:
Length: FL (finished length, or long point) + 4" ÷ 36 = yardage.
For double cascades, double the yardage after the calculations.

Self-lined:
Length: FL (finished length, or long point) x 2 + 4" ÷36 = yardage.

Yardage: Jabots
Allow approximately one third yard of fabric for each jabot.

Special Note
1. See page 102 for detailed calculating terms

Photo & illustration: Multiple board mounted swags. Custom renderings by DreamDraper® design software, www.dreamdraper.com © 2009 Evan Marsh Designs, Inc.

Overlapping swags are draped gracefully across a window, making an elegant and formal statement. A section of draped fabric at the top of the window that typically resembles a sideways "C" shape, a swag is sometimes coupled with a vertical cascade or "tail" which hangs gracefully on either side.

For additional treatments and embellishments, see Appendices beginning on page 288.

Yardage

Swags, plain fabric – 1.5 yards for contrast lined swags up to 40" and 3 yards if self-lined. Two yards for swags between 40" and 60" and 4 yards if self-lined. For swags over 60" consult a professional drapery workroom as these swags may need to be "railroaded" and yardage calculations can be complex.

Things to Consider

> Swag type: Pleated, gathered or boxed
> Color of lining or self-lined
> Window sizes in relation to swags in the same room
> Clearance for French doors
> Returns

Special Notes

1. Swags look best between 30" and 40" wide
2. A re-measure by the workroom is strongly recommended
3. Linear swags are a better choice for bay windows
4. See page 102 for detailed calculating terms

Contemporary Swags

Photo: Single pole mounted swag with contrast lining;
illustration: Multiple pole mounted swags

Swags are draped across the window on a decorative pole and constructed to appear as if the fabric is thrown casually over the rod or constructed as one large swag that is mounted on wood, wrought iron, or medallions.

For additional treatments and embellishments, see Appendices beginning on page 288.

Yardage
One swag
Width of area to be covered + 30% ÷ 36 = yardage
More than one swag:
Width of area to be covered x 1.5 ÷ 36 = yardage

Things to Consider
> Color of lining
> Width and drop of swags
> Number of swags

> Mounting on medallions, wrought iron or poles

Special Notes
1. These swags are usually cut on the straight grain of the fabric. Any fabric with an obvious directional print is not suitable.
2. Proportions are important for this type of swag
3. A check measure by the workroom is highly recommended.
4. For bay windows consult a professional
5. See page 102 for detailed calculating terms

Photo: Board mounted linear swags with cascades; *illustration:* Bullion trimmed board mounted linear swags

These swags are butted together, without overlapping; therefore, they most often require cascades, jabots and/ or rosettes to conceal molding, drapery headings, or unsightly hardware. Linear swags are a good choice for bay windows, where overlapping swags are difficult and inappropriate. Linear swags need not "touch" each other; they can be separated by a few inches, thus saving on yardage and labor, if double cascades are used (*see above*).

For additional treatments and embellishments, see Appendices beginning on page 288.

Yardage

Swags, plain fabric – 1.5 yards for contrast lined swags up to 40" and 3 yards if self-lined. Two yards for swags between 40" and 60" and 4 yards if self-lined. For swags over 60" consult a professional drapery workroom as these swags may need to be "railroaded"

and yardage calculations can be complex.

Things to Consider

> Color of lining, or self lined
> Contrast or self lined jabots, cascades
> Width and length in relations to other windows in the same room
> Number and type of swags
> Returns, if any

Special Notes

1. To achieve proper proportions, consult with workroom.

2. See page 102 for detailed calculating terms

Photo: Empire valance; *illustration:* Kingston valances.

An elaborate valance that gets its fullness form pulling the pleats up to the top of the board, unlike the Kingston that gets its fullness from behind the horns. The Empire valance is usually adorned with horns "jabots" and/ or side cascades.

For additional treatments and embellishments, see Appendices beginning on page 288.

Yardage *(including Empire or Kingston valance)*

Step 1 – BF (board face) + 6" for RT (returns, if going over draperies) x 2.5 ÷ width of fabric = number of widths required (round up to whole number)

Step 2a – FL (finished length) x 2 + 10" for HH (headings and hems) x widths required ÷ 36 = yardage (round up to whole number) without pattern repeat *(or)*

Step 2b – FL (finished length) x 2 + 10" for HH ÷ pattern repeat = number of repeats required (round up to whole number)

Step 2c: – Number of repeats x pattern repeat = CL (cut length)

Step 2d –

Number of widths x CL (cut length) ÷ 36 = yardage with pattern repeat (round up to whole number)

Things to Consider

> Width and length, color of lining

> Mounting: board or decorative rod

Special Notes

1. This is a stationary treatment.

2. This treatment cannot be used if treatment mounted underneath is installed up to the ceiling.

3. Extra yardage has to be calculated for rod covers.

4. See page 102 for detailed calculating terms

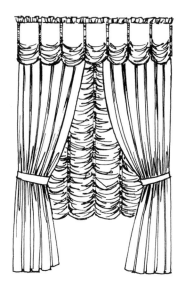

Photo: Outside mounted balloon valance; *illustration:* Balloon valance over pleated draperies and Austrian shade.

This valance has large, inverted pleats that create a more tailored effect than its counterpart, the cloud valance. Used alone or with an undertreatment, its soft look and pretty poufs add a feminine touch.

For additional treatments and embellishments, see Appendices beginning on page 288.

Yardage *(including Balloon or Cloud valance)*

Step 1 – Width of valance + RT (returns) x 2.5 ÷ width of fabric = number of fabric widths required (round up to whole number)

Step 2a – Valance length + 16" for HH (heading and hems) x widths required ÷ 36 = yardage without pattern repeat *(or)*

Step 2b – Valance length + 16" for HH ÷ pattern repeat = number of repeats required (round up whole number)

Step 2c – Number of repeats required x pattern repeat = CL (cut length)

Step 2d – Number of widths x CL ÷ 36 = yardage with pattern repeat (round up to whole number)

Things to Consider

> Width, length and color of lining
> Placement: inside, outside, or ceiling mounted
> Size of returns and mounting: board or rod

Special Notes

1. For valances shorter than 16", a functional balloon that can be raised to the correct height is recommended.
2. See page 102 for detailed calculating terms

Box Pleated Valance

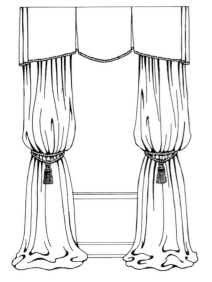

Photo: Contrast lined inverted box pleated valance; *illustration:* Box pleated valance over Bishop sleeve panels

Crisp and tailored, this top treatment lends itself well to pairings with many different kinds of undertreatments, both hard and soft.

For additional treatments and embellishments, see Appendices beginning on page 288.

Yardage *(including Box Pleated, Inverted Box Pleated)*
Step 1 – BFW (board face width) + 6" or 12" for RT (returns) x 2.5 ÷ width of fabric = number of widths required (round up to whole number)
Step 2a – FL (finished length) + 8" for HH (headings and hems) x widths required ÷ 36 = yardage (round up to whole number) without pattern repeat (*or*)
Step 2b – FL (finished length) + 8" for HH ÷ pattern repeat = number of repeats required (round up to whole number)
Step 2c – Number of repeats x pattern repeat = CL (cut length)

Step 2d – Number of widths x CL (cut length) ÷ 36 = yardage with pattern repeat (round up to whole number)

Things to Consider
> Width, length and returns
> Contrast fabric color if "open throat" (*as shown above*)

Special Notes
1. A check measure and installation are strongly recommended.
2. Pleats are sized to window and pattern usually 5" to 16".
3. See page 102 for detailed calculating terms

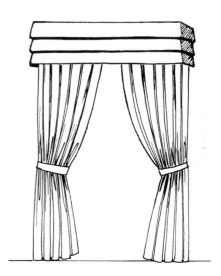

Photo & illustration: Mock Roman valances

This top treatment suggests the look of a Roman shade yet it cannot be raised or lowered. A variety of decorative trims or contrasting bands can be employed to create interest.

For additional treatments and embellishments, see Appendices beginning on page 288.

Yardage

Step 1 – BFW (board face width) + 6" or 12" for RT (returns) + 4" ÷width of fabric = number of widths required (round up to whole number)

Step 2a – FL (finished length) x 2 + 6" for HH (headings and hems) x widths required ÷ 36 = yardage (round up to whole number) without pattern repeat (*or*)

Step 2b – FL (finished length) x 2 + 6" for HH ÷ pattern repeat = number of repeats required (round up to whole number)

Step 2c – Number of repeats x pattern repeat = CL (cut length)

Step 2d – Number of widths x CL (cut length) ÷ 36 = yardage with pattern repeat (round up to whole number)

Things to Consider

> Width, length, color of lining, and returns

> Inside or outside mount

Special Notes

1. See page 102 for detailed calculating terms.

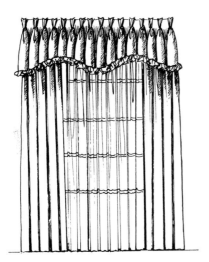

Photo & illustration: Legacy valances

Softly shaped, this valance adds beauty without distorting the view. Unlike the Savannah valance, which is arched, the Legacy valance offers a dip down in the center. In addition, the header may be pleated, shirred or tunneled.

For additional treatments and embellishments, see Appendices beginning on page 288.

Yardage *(including Legacy and Arched valances)*

Step 1 – RFW (rod face width) + 6" or 12" for RT (returns) x 3 ÷ width of fabric = number of widths required (round up to whole number)

Step 2a – FL (finished length) from longest point + 16" for HH (headings and hems) x widths required ÷ 36 = yardage (round up to whole number) without pattern repeat *(or)*

Step 2b – FL (finished length) from longest point + 16" for HH ÷ pattern repeat = number of repeats required (round up to whole number)

Step 2c – Number of repeats x pattern repeat = CL (cut length)

Step 2d – Number of widths x CL (cut length) ÷ 36 = yardage with pattern repeat (round up to whole number)

Things to Consider

> Width and returns

> Longest point, shortest point and mid-point

> Standup or no standup, type of rod

Special Notes

1. A check measure and installation are strongly recommended.

2. Use a hook and loop fastener for shirred headings.

3. See page 102 for detailed calculating terms

Photo: Upholstered cornice; *illustration:* Upholstered lambrequin

General Information: Cornices & Lambrequins

Cornices and lambrequins are padded with polyester fiberfill and constructed of wood or chipboard. Fabric is usually stapled securely to the back side of the cornice, well-hidden from not just the front of the piece but also from underneath.

Non-directional and solid fabrics should be rail-roaded to eliminate seams, matching welt cord is standard on all cornices and is applied to the top and bottom edges. Using a coordinating color for the welting has a more dramatic effect.

When ordering a cornice or lambrequin to fit a tight application (i.e., wall to wall or bay windows, for example) be sure to measure at the elevation of the installation. Exact outside face measurements — wall to wall installation. Also allow one inch for clearance.

For additional treatments and embellishments, see Appendices beginning on page 288.

Measuring

Measure drapery rod from end bracket to end bracket and add four inches for rod clearance and cornice or lambrequin. Six inch returns are needed when mounted over a single rod and eight-inch returns are needed when mounted over a double rod.

Special Note

1. See page 102 for detailed calculating terms.

Photo & illustration: Beautifully embellished upholstered cornices

Design by Diana Apgar, Interiors by Decorating Den; photo by Randy Foulds

Crisp and tailored, this top treatment lends itself well to pairings with many different kinds of undertreatments, both hard and soft.

For additional treatments and embellishments, see Appendices beginning on page 288.

2. Off center prints may create an unbalanced effect, so choose fabric carefully.
3. See page 102 for detailed calculating terms.

Yardage

See chart (adjacent)

Things to Consider

> Width,
> Length: shortest + longest points
> Style
> Fabric details

Special Notes

1. A check measure and installation are strongly recommended.

Cornice Style/Width Chart

Style	Width		
	48" to 84"	84" to 120"	120" to 144"
Tailored	2 yards	3 yards	3.5 yards
Square Notch	2 yards	3 yards	3.5 yards
Scallop	2 yards	3 yards	3.5 yards
Scroll	2 yards	3 yards	3.5 yards
Ruched	3 yards	4.5 yards	5.5 yards

Decorative Hardware & Trims

It is with decorative hardware and trims that the customization and individuality of a window treatment begins. A wonderful emphasis for the shape and form of a treatment, trim is at its most effective when placed along the edge or hem of a drapery or curtain, as well as used as a beautiful punctuation to the bottom of a roller shade, or as a decorative tape to soften the hard edges of a wood blind.

Decorative hardware is another means to add emphasis. With many choices in materials — wrought iron, steel, glass, carved wood and more — to rings, tieback holders, rods, scarf brackets… your choices are many.

Left: Currant red loop fringe plays chicken with the strong, sturdy tweed fabric, a delightful tease of a decorative trim that draws attention, even though it is tone-on-tone. *Above:* Bullion trimmed swag and cascade is divine.

History in the Making

As soon as there was a need, decorative hardware made its appearance. From the most rustic of wooden rods used to suspend a flimsy burlap panel centuries ago to the heavy wrought iron beauties of today, hardware has evolved from mere necessity into eye-catching focal points.

As for passementerie — or in simple terms, decorative trimmings — it has long been a sign of wealth and social status to embellish a drapery treatment, piece of furniture, the rim of a lamp shade or even the bottom of a picture frame, with braid, bullion, beads and especially, tassels of every shape and size. Ornate tassels can range from the extremely expensive and available only through an interior design professional, to simple adornments that can be made at home in five or ten minutes with just a skein of yarn and a piece of heavy cardboard.

Left: Decorative tassels are a luxurious means to turn an ordinary window treatment into something extraordinary.

Above: Luscious bullion fringe, tassels and cornice make this treatment stand out.

Today's Decorative Hardware & Trims

Today, the choices are endless. Delicate edging marries with beads, feathers, tassels and tiebacks to form beautiful works of window art. Use a contrasting color for a dramatic look; a tone-on-tone trim for a subtle accent. Place tiebacks according to the "one-third" rule — either one-third from the bottom of the treatment, or one-third from the top — but never halfway.

But it is in the application, too, that many a treatment fails. Too much trim will cheapen a treatment, too little will look like an effort wasted. If you are in doubt, be sure to talk to your interior design professional. Other than that, enjoy the unique qualities that decorative hardware and trims can bring to your home.

This elaborate cornice plays host to a variety of trimmings from large and small decorative tassels to cording.
Design by Rebecca Shearn, Interiors by Decorating Den

The Facts: Decorative Hardware & Trims

Advantages: Adds a custom, unique element of individuality to any treatment; enhances the visual, as well as the aesthetic, appeal of a room; the perceived and actual value of a window treatment increases with the addition of decorative hardware and trimmings; can provide a focal point

Disadvantages: Too much trim can overwhelm a treatment; too heavy a trim can cause a treatment to sag and stretch; the wrong style of hardware can overwhelm a delicate treatment — and a too delicate set of hardware can be lost within a heavy, formal treatment.

Cost: Can vary depending upon the type and material. Simple rods can be acquired for around $20 but can increase considerably for more ornate detailing and materials; as for trimmings, a simple key tassel starts at about five dollars but a large, bead encrusted tassel is upwards of $100 or more.

Lifespan: Years+

Most Appropriate Locations: Decorative hardware and trim is appropriate on any treatment; it is the placement and style of the trim that makes the difference. In areas of high moisture, consider a glass bead versus a fringe or fabric-style trim

Care & Cleaning: Check the edges of your window treatment (where it may be handled most frequently) for wear and soiling. Re-sew beads that have come loose, spot clean according to manufacturer's directions. Many dry cleaning services will not guarantee that beads and other embellishments will not come loose with cleaning (such as with a wedding dress)—especially when those trims have been attached with hot glue rather than sewn down.

Left: Decorative hardware and trimmings: the icing on the cake!

Above: Abundant bullion fringe plays hide and seek with deep pleats, held in place with beautiful metallic rod and rings.
Design by Suzanne Price, Interiors by Decorating Den

Below: A basketweave finial draws attention to lovely goblet pleats accented with decorative tape.

The Window Decorating Book

Left: Lavish brush fringe lines this drapery panel elegantly. Note how the tassel tiebacks are attached via a small hook on the wall. This is a quick and unobtrusive way to contain the tieback when needed and easy also to release when you wish to cover your window.

Right: This seashore-style window treatment celebrates the water stylishly with seashell holdbacks as well as grommets tied with jaunty rope. From the blue and white fabric, reminiscent of water and waves, to the nautical hardware, this treatment does everything right.

Below: Tie top; Traditional ring and rod header with stitched in rings; Shower curtain-style ring and rod; tab top; Grommet top with rings; In-and-out grommet drapery header.

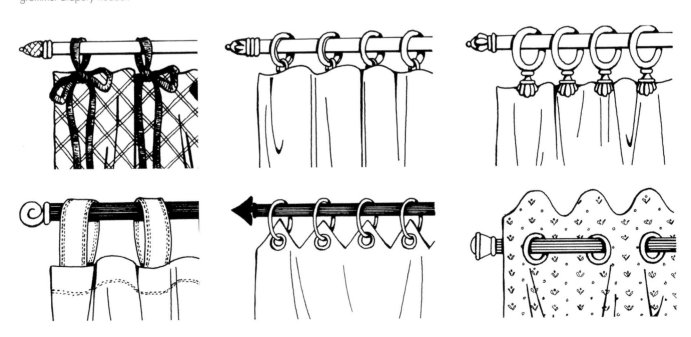

Decorative Hardware & Trims

Good to Know: Passementerie

Passementerie, also known as trimming, is available many different ways.

Ball fringe: Small balls (such as a pom-pom or even beaded balls) are attached to a flat, raw edge that will be inserted into a seam before it is closed up. A more casual look.

Braid: Similar to gimp (*see definition next page*), braid is used primarily to conceal raw edges and seams.

Brush fringe: A more casual look than bullion, the brush fringe looks very similar to its moniker: like a soft, downy brush. When purchased, the brush fringe will have a long strand of protective chain stitches holding the fringe in place. This thread is removed after its installation onto the treatment is complete.

Bullion: Long, twisted lengths of rope form a dense fringe. Typically five inches or longer, it is a lush edging for heavier fabric (such as velvet) draperies, although it can be lighter and more casual. It has taken over ruffles as a more popular way to edge a treatment.

Button: A decorative accent, typically covered with fabric or woven cord, used to provide a small indentation in an upholstered piece such as a cornice or more often, a pillow or arm of an upholstered chair.

Cord: Created by twisting or braiding, a cord can be made of a variety of colors and fibers. Typically employed as an edging for upholstery but can also be used to edge a very heavy drapery panel. Has a "lip" to allow ease of attachment in between seams.

Tone-on-tone trimming is sophisticated and elegant against these silk drapery panels.

Edging: A decorative piece that has one raw edge and one embellished edge.

Eyelash fringe: Named because the short, tiny fringe resembles eyelashes.

Fringe: Available in sizes from about one inch in length to about eighteen inches, fringe is a lighter style of bullion: whereas the bullion is more like twisted rope, fringe is more like multiple threads. Can also be a length of delicate tassels, a row of balls or even beads.

Frog: A two-piece closure made of cord that is wound in a decorative manner. One half of the frog houses the loop; the other houses the knot. Used for decoration.

Gimp: A thin, woven braid typically used to cover seams or to mask upholstery tacks or staples. Usually silk or metallic, it is finished on both edges. Can be stitched on or glued.

Key tassel: A small, decorative tassel used for accentuating.

Lipcord: A decorative cord to which a narrow piece of fabric (the lip) has been attached. That fabric is slid into an open area (to be seamed) during the construction of a drapery. When the seam is stitched, the cord covers the seamed area, concealing it.

Loop fringe: Similar to brush fringe, only the fringe loops back into the finial or lip cord rather than it being cut at the bottom.

Piping: A thin cord covered in fabric that is used primarily to cover seams.

Rick rack: Typically a serpentine-shaped, thin flat braid used for edging, such as on dotted Swiss curtains.

Rosette: A detailing fabric piece used primarily for accentuating. Resembles a flower and can be quite large when used

Evoking spring, pink and green will always be fresh and in style. This lively combination is at once gloriously distinctive and openly welcoming.

at the top of a drapery, or quite small, such as when used to dot the side of an upholstered chair. Can also showcase a tassel hanging from the middle.

Tassel: Consisting of three main parts: the cord (used to suspend the tassel), the top (holds the fringe in place, can also be called a finial) and the skirt (the fringe that hangs from inside the top of the piece), a tassel can range from very simple (such as a key tassel) to extremely heavy and ornate. Can either have a "cut" skirt (the yarn is trimmed at the bottom) or a looped skirt, in which the yarn loops down from the finial and then back up inside.

Tieback: A shaped piece of fabric or cording used to pull a drapery panel away from a window.

Previous page: Tab top stationary panels in a golden toile pattern flank this French door, hanging from elegantly short metallic rods.

Above: Gimp and beaded fringe are exceptionally lovely. What an exquisite treat to have in a home!

Decorative Hardware & Trims

Bead Trim

Bracket

Braid/Welt Cord

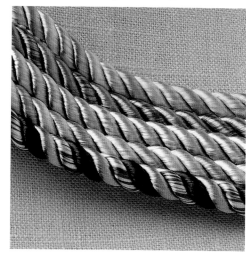

Decorative Tape

Finial-Glass

Finial-Metal

Decorative Hardware & Trim

Some of the more common decorative hardware styles include:

Upper row, left: Bead trim can be made of many different materials: glass, wood, etc.
Upper row, middle: A bracket holds a rod in place.
Upper row, right: Braid/welt cord is used to edge fabric and seams.
Middle row, left: Decorative tape is an upgrade to add beauty to blinds and fabric.
Middle row, middle: Glass finials can catch the light — and the eye — with their beauty.
Middle row, right: Metal finials provide a modern appearance.
Bottom row: Wood finials are solid and permanent looking.

Next page:
Upper row, left: Brush fringe is soft and lush.
Upper row, middle: Bullion fringe is weighty and best used on heavier drapery materials.
Upper row, right: Grommets are a mod way to hang a drapery.
Middle row, left: Holdbacks pull draperies aside and are found in both fabric and solid materials.
Middle row, middle: Medallion/end caps can cap off a rod in style.
Middle row, right: Ring and rod arrangements are a very traditional way to hang draperies.
Lower row, left: Rosettes provide beautiful accents.
Lower row, middle: Shade pulls keep hands off the beautiful shade material.
Lower row, right: Tassels are used in many ways — as accents, pulls and edging, etc.

Finial-Wood

Fringe-Brush

Fringe-Bullion

Grommet

Holdback

Medallion/End Cap

Ring & Rod

Rosette

Shade Pull

Tassel

Decorative Hardware

While hardware falls into two categories: the visual and the non-visual, you can't have a window treatment without it. Beautiful hardware makes your window treatment unique and eye-catching.

Baton: A long wand that attaches to the top edge of a drapery. Its main function is to offer an easy way to traverse draperies back and forth without having to touch (and thus, possibly soil) the fabric. Usually, it is hidden in the folds of the draperies when opened and also hangs behind the drapery, rather than in front.

Bracket: Typically an indiscrete piece of hardware, the bracket holds the drapery rod in place. Sometimes it is visible, such as at the end of a pole where it is a point of emphasis, but most often, the bracket is a piece of hardware best left hidden.

Finial: A decorative hardware piece attached to the end of a pole or rod, which keeps the drapery from falling off the end.

Holdback: A piece of hardware placed about one-third to midway between the top and bottom of a window, used to hold draperies back to either side. Typically used in conjunction with a tieback.

Ring: There are different uses for the ring, a circular hardware piece available in many different sizes and materials. When small, it is used in conjunction with a rod and helps the drapery traverse. Used in combination with a drapery hook, which is hidden inside of a pinch pleat at the top of the drapery, for example. When used in a larger format, it can become a bracket used to sling a scarf treatment through or offer some type of containment for holding a part of the drapery. Typically, the larger format ring is stationary.

Rod: A straight piece of drapery hardware usually made of wood, polymer or a metal such as wrought iron or steel that is suspended between two points through the use of brackets or rod end holders. Attached at the top of a window frame, or even further up yet at ceiling level, the drapery rod is the foremost piece of hardware used to suspend a window treatment.

Left: Hanging draperies at ceiling level enhances the feeling of a room's height — especially effective when it is particularly wide. Additionally, the stunning drapery hardware, in this case, heavy black rods enhanced with metallic details, are eye-catching — another way to pull the eye up and around the interior.

Above: This stunning piece of drapery hardware is used as a holdback. In essence, the fabric panel is tucked behind it. It would also be useful as a scarf bracket, one in which the scarf could drape across it if mounted at the top of a window frame. The detailing on this piece of hardware is beautiful and would add a unique beauty to any décor.

Decorative Hardware & Trims

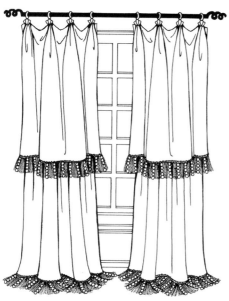

Top left: An ordinary matchstick shade was made extraordinary through the copious use of trims and decorative tassel. These subtle, elegant details elevate a product to art.

Bottom left: Shower-style ring and rod hung panels are doubled up to draw the eye to the center of the treatment, showcasing intricate fringe and bead trim.

Top right: Metallics are still a very popular tone in any space. Here, fine curves enhance this rod and finial combination, so well-designed in its simplicity.

Bottom right: Cuffed panel valances over drapery panels provide and unusual look. The longer far endge of the valance pull the eye down and allow it to focus on the puddled fabric and trims on the floor.

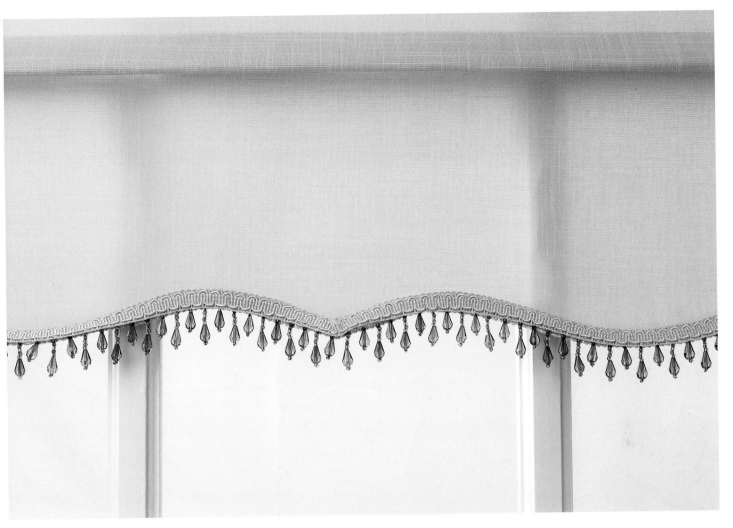

Above: Delicate bead trim with tone-on-tone gimp takes an average roller shade and makes it magnificent.

Right: Long bead trim is light but perfectly suited for this swag and tail treatment, enhancing the folds but not weighing them down or overpowering the look.

The Window Decorating Book

Previous page:

Above left: Tiny tassel trim lines the edge of this balloon shade, drawing attention away from the hard treatment behind it.

Below left: A pretty crackle finish enhances the look of this drapery finial, aging it slightly for an Old World feel.

Below right: The detailing on this small-scale finial provides an unobtrusive, elegant look, so pretty, it's almost a shame to cover it with fabric and rings!

This page below: This metallic drapery hardware is a terrific complement to the out of doors. Notice how one first looks at the autumn leaves outside the French doors before eyes come to rest at the magnificent holdback, then up to the rod and rings above the door. This window treatment, in general, is a terrific and more unusual way to treat an egress area. It's very ceremonial to draw the draperies at night. To cover a door in this way is the ultimate in tucking in for the night.

This page right: A short decorative rod with finials enhance a simple tied back panel. Custom rendering by DreamDraper® design software, www.dreamdraper.com © 2009 Evan Marsh Designs, Inc.

Consider This: Trims & Tassels

- In the jewelry world, the rule is to put on your jewels: your earrings, necklace, bracelet, brooch — whatever you want to wear for the evening — and then remove one item. It is the tasteful arrangement of beauty upon beauty that makes not only the wearer shine, but also what she is wearing. The same rule holds true for decorative trimmings and tassels. Too much passementerie: too many beads, too many rows of fringe, too many tiebacks, gimp, braids and more, can make a mess of a beautiful treatment. Choose your trims sparingly, and you will not be disappointed.

- Not all passementerie is formal. The wide variety of trims makes it possible to accentuate in countless ways: masculine, exotic, regal, fanciful, pretty, modern. The type of trim you select can set or enhance a mood and also tie together disparate elements.

- Plan your trims carefully. A good rule is to choose a trim color that complements the main fabric, and is also consistent with its style and treatment shape. Tone-on-tone coloration, however, is also very beautiful in its sublety. Don't rule out that a deep burgundy trim on a deep burgundy drapery won't work well or pop — consider that the sheen may be different and that the trim will display well due to heightened light reflection off of its threads.

Left: Coordinating trims and tassels are an outstanding way to draw attention to an area within your interior.

Above: Lush tassels secure a window treatment with style. When ready to close the draperies at night, just unhook the tassel cord from its holdback and let the drapes fall across your window.

Right: Contrast trim draws attention to the edge of this silk panel, a pretty detail.

Below: Lush, elaborate bullion fringe and multiple tassels enhance goblet pleated panel.

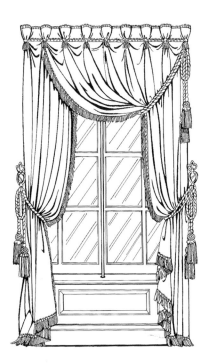

Above: Metal beads offer an unusual pop of interest on this sheer shade treatment; pretty gimp on the edge provides a visual line between the shade and beads. Design by Suzanne Price, Interiors by Decorating Den

Upper, middle and lower left: Unique and intricate finial designs will elevate a drapery rod to the upper end of style. Notice the beautiful carved details on the round, middle finial, for example, or the regal flair of the lower finial. The drapery finial is an extension of the treatment's style and should be given as much thought as any other part of the design.

Below: Exceptional stationary drapery panels are swagged from individual scarf brackets. Dripping with bullion fringe, each panel offers a unique solution. Notice how the center treatment spans the corner — a particularly difficult area to treat. Design by Rebecca Shearn, Interiors by Decorating Den

Upper left: Over-the-top decorative flowers become a focal point in this girl's bedroom, offering both flirty style along with the means to swag the drapery panels away from the window.

Upper right: Huge yellow tassels on the sheer drapery treatments are designed to play off of the large floral motifs and tie in with the wall color.
Design by Suzanne Price, Interiors by Decorating Den

Lower left: Pony beads intertwine with larger scale coin pearl beads to offer a unique fringe. Note that the beads are more than likely installed onto a lipcord or piece of edging that is slid into the area to be seamed during the construction process. Once the seam is closed, it looks as if each strand was attached individually.

Lower right: Metal floral scarf brackets mounted at ceiling level hold the tabs of this tent-fold treatment in place. Note the decorative buttons, used as the means to secure the contrast fabric back — a cute touch.

Above: Simple tassel tiebacks are an understated means to accent these stylish panels and also provide a means to let the sunshine in during the day.

Left: A simple shade becomes a luscious treat with the addition of short bullion fringe.

Right: This very formal Kingston treatment with Italian strung undershade displays gorgeous tassel trim punctuated with gold studs along the trim edge. While not for just any home, this period piece is picture perfect in its execution of detail.

Below: Fleur de lys holdbacks release the fringe trimmed panels easily. Custom rendering by DreamDraper® design software, www.dreamdraper.com © 2009 Evan Marsh Designs

Above: Delicate beads follow a graceful line along the edge of the treatment.

The Window Decorating Book

Upper: On the same window treatment as the one across the page, feathered tassels pull the drapery panel back from the window.

Middle: Larger cloth trim with matching tassel is a less formal look. Design by Lorraine Brown, Interiors by Decorating Den; photo by Randy Foulds

Lower left: Brown and blue beads with gimp edge the drapery and provide a grounding weight. Design by Sheryl McLean, Interiors by Decorating Den; photo by Randy Foulds

Below: Intricate tassel with ribbons matches well with the beautifully patterned drapery panel.

Left: A heavier tassel and braid add grandeur.

Top left: Pretty, delicate gimp and beading add a unique touch. Design by Barbara Elliott/Jennifer Ward Woods, Interiors by Decorating Den; photo by Jeff Sanders

Bottom left: Elaborately pleated cascades tumble down the sides of the stationary drapery panels, enhanced by the three part swag above.

Top right: Could there be anything prettier at the window? Delicate passementerie is accented by the tassel tieback. Design by Lisa Landry, Interiors by Decorating Den; photo by Ken Vaughn

Bottom right: Decorative rod over pleated draperies with attached flags. Custom rendering by DreamDraper® design software, www.dreamdraper.com © 2009 Evan Marsh Designs

Above: A carefully wrapped tassel lies beautifully against the silk drapery panel.

Left: Simple yet elegant, the wine-tone tassel harmonizes well with the patterned fabric.

Right: Gold tassels on chocolate brown provide a pop of contrast.

Below: Instead of hiding the shape of this grand window, a drapery treatment was chosen to accent its graceful arch. Tassel detailing is an inspired choice.

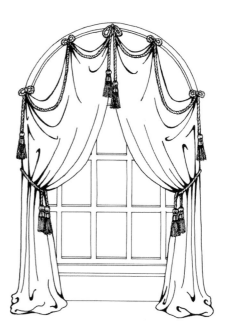

Above: The hard edges of the metal holdback are a terrific contrast to the soft sheer panel.

The Window Decorating Book

Upper right: How simple — use a sturdy ribbon to hold back a sheer in a charming manner.

Lower right: These intricately woven tassels provide a magnificent pop of elegance.

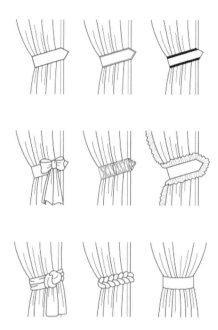

Photo: Simple fabric tieback; *illustrations:* Variety of tieback details

Tiebacks

This decorative accent is used to hold draperies and curtains back from the window. Of course, they can be released from their wall-mounted hook or hold-back in order to allow fabric to fall back against the window. There are many, many different styles to choose from. Shown above is probably the most simple of the bunch: a standard tieback.

For additional treatments and embellishments, see Appendices beginning on page 288.

Yardage

Standard – 1/2 yard
Standard with piping –1/2 yard + 1/2 yard piping
Standard with bandin – 1/2 yard + 1/2 yard banding
Standard with bows – 1/2 yard + one yard bows
Contour – 3/4 yard
Ruched tieback – 1 yard

Ruffled tieback – 1 yard + 1.5 yard ruffle
Streamer tieback – 2 yards
Braided tieback – 1/2 yard each strand (three strands)
Collar with hook and loop fastene – 1/2 yard

Work Order Specifications

> Style
> Fabric

Special Note

1. See page 102 for detailed calculating terms

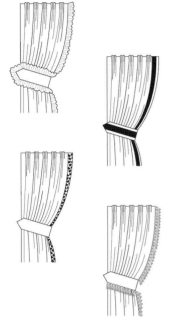

Photo: Silk flower detail clipped to ring; *illustrations:* Variety of details

Adding Personal Touches

There are many details that can be added to personalize a window treatment. Ruffles, for example, add charm and romance to the feeling a room encompasses. Use them on draperies, cushions, tiebacks or comforters for a country-style look.

Inset banding, a band of fabric two-inches or more, is sewn inset from the edges, adding dramatic contrast.

Reverse lining is a decorative facing sewn into the lining, then folded outward to reveal the contrast and is held in place with tiebacks.

Fringe and braid can be used decoratively on a window treatment or other room accessories to echo the elegance of a past era. Even a touch of silk floral, as shown above, will draw the eye.

For additional treatments and embellishments, see Appendices beginning on page 288.

Yardage

Ruffles – 1/4 yard for each 24" of ruffles
Inset banding – Length and hem allowances
Reverse lining – Length and hem allowances
Fringe and braids – Length + additional 10%

Things to Consider

> Treatment
> Fabrics

Special Note

1. See page 102 for detailed calculating terms

Alternatives

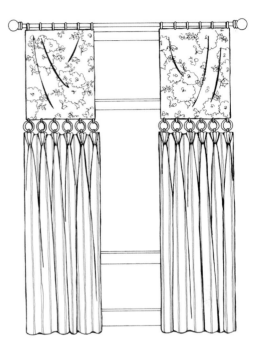

When it comes to window treatments, anything goes — **as far** and as wide as your imagination can take you. Don't want to be like everyone else? Want something unusual? Beyond individualizing your treatments with the vast variety of decorative hardware and trims, consider using unconventional materials as another way to set yourself apart from the others and "up" your cool factor. Window treatments are being made from just about any material: leather, beads, screens and more.

And don't discount the imaginative experimentation one can have with a themed room — one that could, alternately, remind you of a trip to Mardi Gras, a week spent in Italy, or perhaps something as simple as a favorite sports team.

Here's a look.

Left: Panel track systems are a terrific alternative to vertical blinds when treating a sliding glass door area. They are neat and compact — yet note that the stackback will be as wide as one panel.

Above: Multiple fabric panels separated with rings.

Alternative Treatments

Beads

The groovy bead curtain of the 1960s and 1970s has evolved into a sophisticated treatment at the window.

- Advantages: Bead colors can reflect light and provide a rainbow of colors splashed across a room; briolette cut beads can reflect light beautifully; can be used in conjunction with a hard treatment such as a shade or blind.
- Disadvantages: For decoration only. A bead curtain does not provide anything to a room except enhanced aesthetics.

Decorative Enhancers

Enhancers, such as decorative arches constructed of wrought iron or stained glass, provide a pretty look.

- Advantages: A unique way to treat a window, enhancements will play with entering light, filtering and reflecting rays and creating patterns across a room.
- Disadvantages: Usually for decoration only. While some stained glass treatments will filter light, most decorative enhancers are for beauty only.

Leather

Like traditional fabric, leather is adaptable, pliable and also an unusual look at the window. The difference in each individual animal hide will make each window treatment inimitable due to its unique markings and measurements.

Instead of covering a window arch completely, consider ironwork to decorate and enhance an architectural element.

- **Advantages:** Room darkening capabilities are exceptional; rustic look makes it perfect for western-style interiors; beadwork or leather fringe can be added to make your treatment even more distinctive; can be around moisture.
- **Disadvantages:** Color variations are limited to about 20 dye tones; no animal hide is alike in size or shape in that each will have some natural markings and holes, such as from insect bites or from rubbing against posts; leather will fade when exposed to direct sunlight; somewhat expensive: a simple swag/jabot treatment starts at about $500.

Shoji Screens

A lightweight, transparent panel originally used in Japanese homes to divide up an interior space, shoji (pronounced "show-gee") screens slide on wooden tracks placed at top and bottom. Today they are used as room dividers, window treatments, skylight covers, cabinet doors and more.

- **Advantages:** Simple, clean lines; can be motorized; easy construction allows adaptability to just about any unusual space issue; fabric instead of screening can be inserted to allow greater flexibility in coordinating room design elements; costs about the same

A lightweight, transparent panel, shoji screens can be used as room dividers (as seen in this application) and also as lovely window treatments.

as a traditional drapery panel.

• Disadvantages: Be sure your screen is made of a stronger hardwood (such as ramin) than an earlier counterpart, which was typically made of cedar or spruce. Also, the rice paper insert can be very fragile, so ask for a more durable material such as laminated rice paper, which is also offered. Somewhat unyielding in terms of privacy issues — the treatment is either open or closed. There is no "in-between" in terms of a bottom up/top down feature.

"Theme" Treatments

Themed window treatments can be found in any area of the home, but none more frequently than in a child's room. Sports-related window treatments and décor schemes are a frequent request, followed by cartoon characters and more whimsical floral, animal and doll-related decorations. But themed treatments are not just for kids. Some homeowners are requesting treatments that remind them of a particular vacation spot they once visited, and there is always a kitchen or two (hundred!) with the proverbial chicken and rooster theme.

• Advantages: Especially for children, a themed window treatment provides joy and individuality to a room; can provide cohesion within a room; can be inexpensive (such as racing pennants waving from a simple rod).

• Disadvantages: As with any theme, the occupants of the room will inevitably tire of this treatment much sooner than something more straightforward; once the theme has run its course, it typically has no further use and must be removed; can be costly — this is not a treatment that will stay up for a lengthy period of time (such as in a child's room).

Left: A spartan panel track on a window wall is a nice way to add a vertical element to a room without taking up much space.

Above: The difference in each individual animal hide will make a leather window treatment inimitable due to its unique markings and measurements.

Below: In this tiny window, a Mardi Gras theme was envisioned and brought to great fruition.

A safari theme in this sitting room is over-the-top adventurous. Everything about this room blends together perfectly, from the animal themed wood and fabric cornice and draperies to the woven wood shade, animal print lampshade and safari artifacts atop the cornice.

An expanse of window covered neatly with sliding sunscreen panels.

Appendix 1

Curtains & Draperies

There are so many possibilities for beautiful curtains and draperies: in these pages you will find additional ideas to inspire you. Note, too, the beautiful embellishments used on these designs, from simple banding techniques to rosettes to tassels to bullion fringe and more. Be sure to decide first upon the shape and style you want, then add the details.

Flat panel draperies with ties on decorative rod

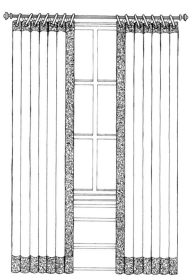

Flat panel draperies with grommets and banding on decorative rod

Flat panel draperies with bullion fringe hems on decorative rod

Flat panel draperies with rosettes, with medallion holdbacks

Puddled stationary panels, held back with fabric ties

Rod top draperies on decorative pole

Pole swag with panels and plentiful passementerie detailing

Drapery folded over decorative rod with rope ties and key tassels

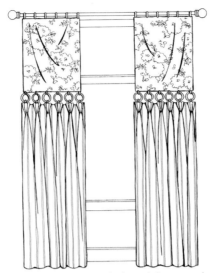

Flat panels over pinch pleated drapery with sew on rings

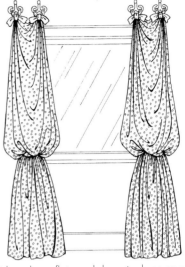

Bishop sleeve flat panel draperies hung on wall brackets

Arched drapery with tassels

Multi fabric rod pocket draperies on swing out decorative rods

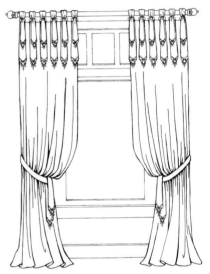

Gathered tab top draperies with double ties over tied back draperies

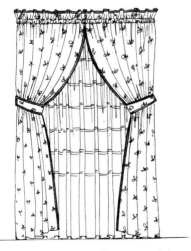

Rod pocket tie backs with ruffle at top and sheer undertreatment

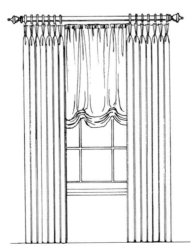

French pleated draperies on decorative rod over balloon shade

Flip topper panels cinched with bands*

Curtains & Draperies

Goblet pleated arch top, puddled with medallion holdbacks*

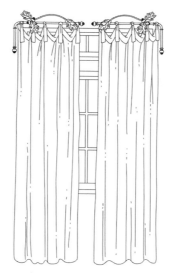

Tie top panels on swing out drapery hardware*

Banded cascades with medallion holdbacks*

Puddled tab top panel with mock cloud valance*

Tab top with contrast banding*

Simple portiere with triangle flags*

Goblet pleated panels with bullion fringe and fleur de lis holdbacks*

Puddled stationary panels with designer headers*

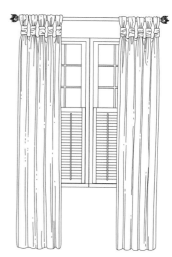

Shirred tab top over shutters*

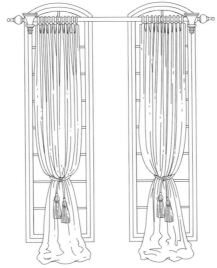

Puddled flip-topper*

Ribbon topped Bishop sleeve*

Shirred goblet pleated with ribbon tieback*

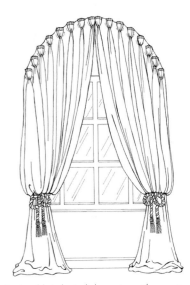

Multi-fabric pinch pleated draperies

Swags with rosettes over puddled draperies

Arched goblet pleated draperies with rope ties

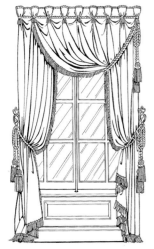

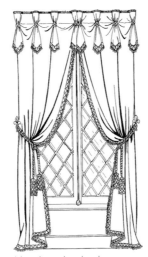

Goblet pleated with bullion fringe

Goblet pleated with jabot accents

String top panels with fabric tiebacks

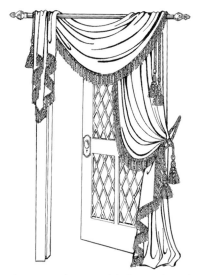

Asymmetrical swag with bullion and tassels

Pencil pleated panels with sheer undertreatment

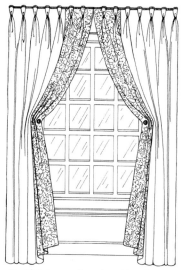

Dual-fabric panels with goblet pleats

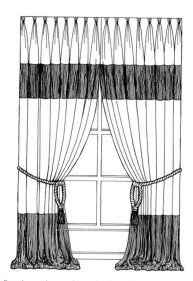

Butterfly pleated panels, color blocked and puddled

Goblet pleats with jabot accent

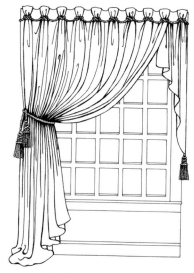

Asymmetrical goblet pleated panels with cascade

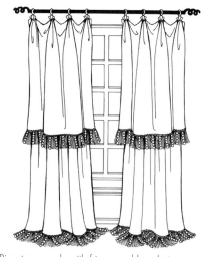

Ring top panels with fringe and bead trim accent

Puddled blouson panels

Grommet topped panels with slight puddle

Color blocked tab top panels

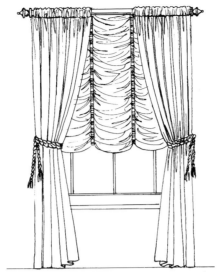

Rod pockets on decorative pole over Austrian shade

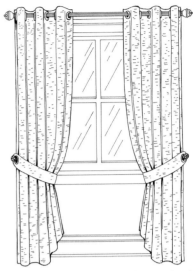

Grommet topped panels with fabric tiebacks

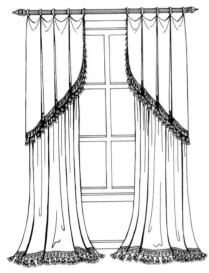

Cuffed panel valances over drapery panels

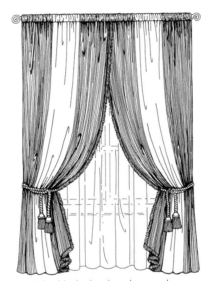

Color blocked rod pocket panels

Knotted tab top panels

Designer swagged panels with tassel detailing

Stationary cuffed panels hung from metal holdbacks

Drapeable panels hung from metal holdbacks

Appendix 2

Fabric Shades

There are so many possibilities for beautiful fabric shades: Roman, London, Austrian and all of the variations thereof. In these pages you will find additional ideas to inspire you. Note, too, the beautiful embellishments used on these designs, from simple banding techniques to rosettes to tassels to bullion fringe and more. Be sure to decide first upon the shape and style you want, then add the details.

Flat Roman shade with center banding and button

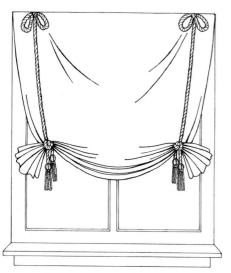

Flat Roman shade with tassels

Balloon shade

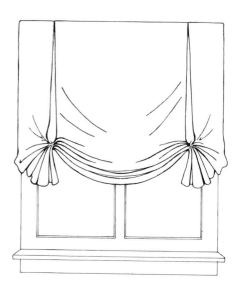

London shade

Roman shade with fabric blocking on every other pleat

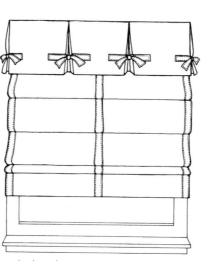

Roman shade with contrast stripes and inverted pleat valance with bow embellishment

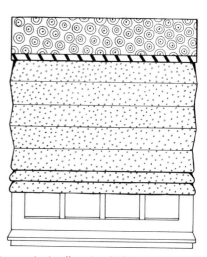

Roman shade offers cheerful fabric combinations

294   The Window Decorating Book

Shirred cloud shade with matching blouson valance

Rod gathered cloud shade with gathered valance

Flat Roman shade with scalloped gathered valance

Roman shade with unique tab top and contrast trim

Flar Roman shade with rod pocket flag accents

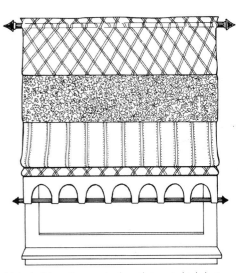

Multiple fabric Roman shade with inverted tab bottom

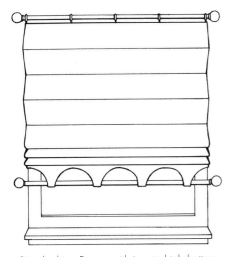

Ring/rod top Roman with inverted tab bottom

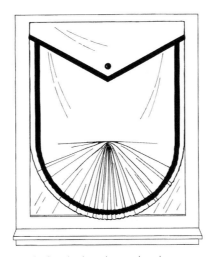

Specialty fan shade with triangle valance top

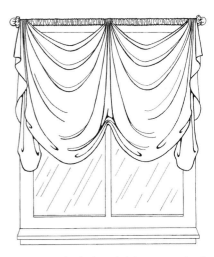

Soft swag-style shade with fabric covered rod

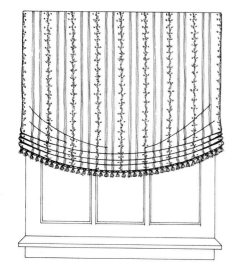

Flat Roman shade

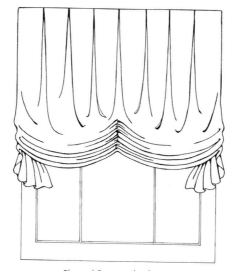

Pleated Roman shade

Pleated balloon shade

Tab Top flat Roman

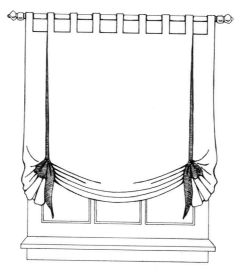

Flat Roman

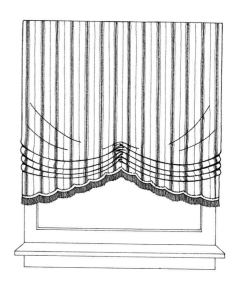

Flat, shirred Roman

London shade

Pleated Roman

Invisibly mounted cloud shade

Rod pocket specialty soft shade

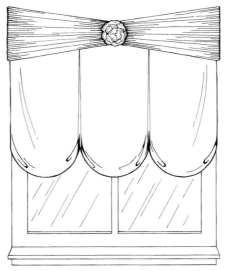

Turban swag cornice atop classic balloon shade

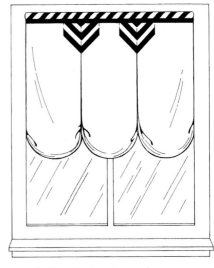

Balloon shade with triangle accents

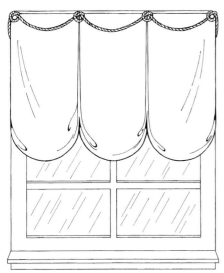

Pleated balloon shade with braid trim

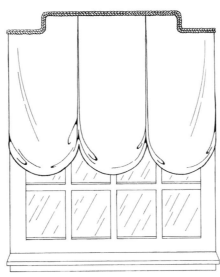

Balloon shade with cut-out corners

Shirred cloud shade with wood cornice

Patterned Roman shade with triangle valance

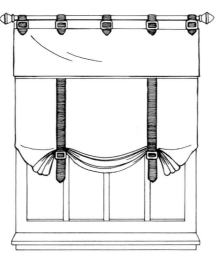

Flat Roman shade with buckle tab tops and straps

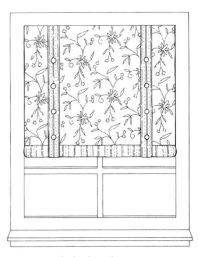

Stagecoach shade with contrast straps

Appendix 3

Combinations

There are so many possibilities for combinations. Basically, take any selection of treatment — at least two — and combine to add volume, take care of a variety of needs and of course, multiply the beauty. Note, too, the beautiful embellishments used on these designs, from simple banding techniques to rosettes to tassels to bullion fringe and more. Be sure to decide first upon the primary look you want, add secondary treatments to finish and then cap the concoction with decorative hardware and trim.

Swags and cascades with medallions, tassels and trim

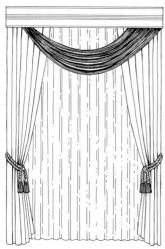

Arched swags over draperies with center flag and tassel

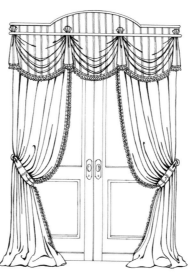

Swagged cornice with wood molding over tied back draperies

Double cascades over cornice box

Wood cornice, sheer underdrapery, side panels with single swag

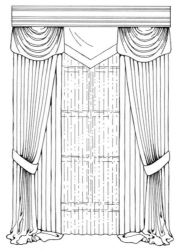

Six parts: wood cornice, sheer underdraperies, overdraperies, side panels, swags, triangle valance

Elaborate swag, jabot and cascade, soft cornice, drapery panels and sheer undertreatment

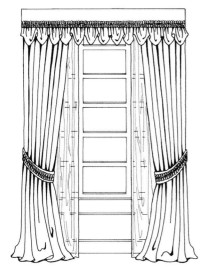

Bloused top treatment with sheer underdraperies and pleated panels

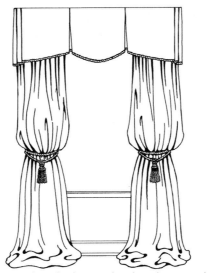

Box pleated valance with Bishop sleeve panels

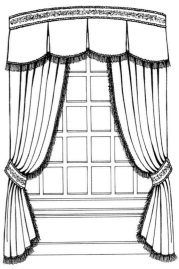

Arched box pleated valance and matching panels

Color blocked panels, inverted box pleat valance

Arched Austrian valance with stationary panels

Triple swags with scarf panels and decorative hardware

Soft cornice with rosette details, stationary panels

Cornices, swags and Bishop sleeve panels

Checkerboard upholstered cornice with puddled panels

Combinations

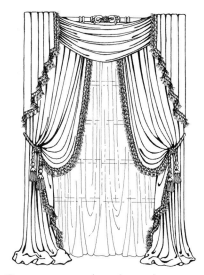

Open swag, cascades with trim, decorative
rod, tieback with tassels

Arched specialty cornice with large rope bows
over draperies

Open tab swags, decorative rod, tie-back
with rope tassels

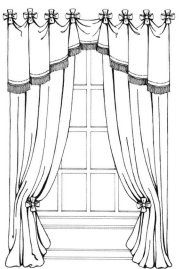

Arched specialty valance with Maltese cross
bows, and Maltese holdbacks

Swag and cascades with rosettes and specialty trim

Double swags with double drapery panels

Arched soft cornice with large buttons over
puddled draperies

Pleated valance with swags and rosettes over
tied-back draperies with rosettes

Gathered tab top draperies over
roller shade

The Window Decorating Book

Open swags with handkerchief flags and rosettes

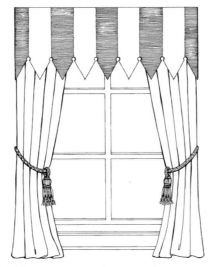

Multi-fabric cornice over draperies with rope ties and tassels

Swag flags over pinch pleated draperies with small tassel fringe

Euro pleated draperies with swags and cascades

Wood cornice over specialty valance with cascades

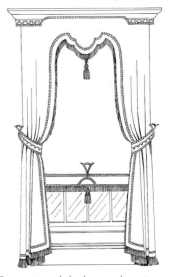

Fringe trimmed shade, wood cornice and stationary panels

Sheers, side panels, wood cornice and soft valance

Swags, cascades and drapery panels

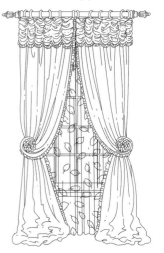

Puddled panels under blouson valance with sheer floral underdraperies*

Combinations

Wood cornice, scalloped swags and
drapery panels

Wood cornice, swags, cascades and panels

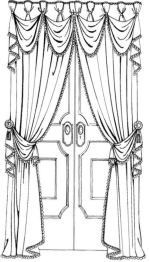

Goblet pleated panels, swags and cascades

Sheer undertreatment, double drapery panels
and wood cornice

Pole swag with rod pocket and short valance

Empire valance accented with pleated panels

Contrast band empire valance with
pleated panels

Swag and jabot with cascades and
simple draperies

Swag and cascade with
uncomplicated panels

The Window Decorating Book

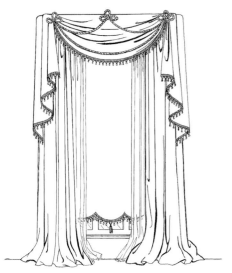

Scalloped fabric shade with swag and puddled panels

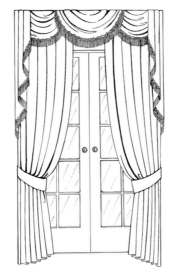

Board mounted swag with tied back panels

Three part swag with pleated cascade and panels

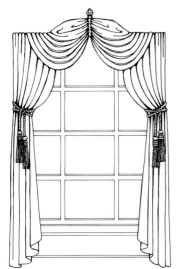

Board mounted swag with panel accents

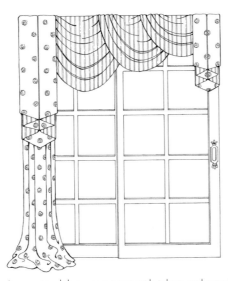

Asymmetrical three part swag with jabots and panel

Soft swag and jabot cornice with puddled panels

Sheer undretreatment, swags, cascades and panels

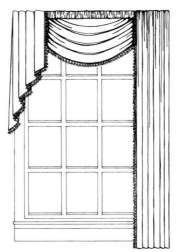

Swag and pleated cascade, fabric covered rod and stationary panel

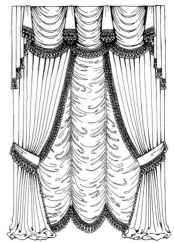

Kingston valance, Italian strung underdraperies, and drapery panels

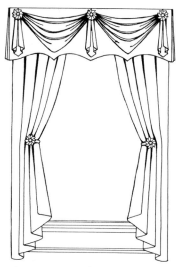

Soft cornice, triangular swags and jabots, panels

Swag and cascades, sheer undertreatment, heavy panels

Swag and cascade with panels and matching tiebacks

Swag and jabot top with sheers and panels

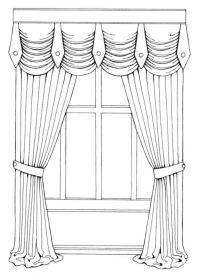

Empire valance with jabots, wood cornice and side panels

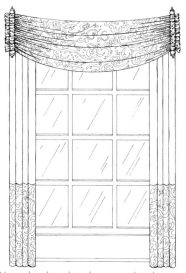

Vertical rod pocketed swag with side panels

Slouchy swag and cascade over puddled panels

Sheer side panel with pole swags

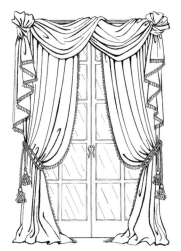

Pole swag with decorative knots, cascades and panels

Sheer swag, cascade and side panel

Goblet pleated legacy valance with lush panels

Goblet pleated panels with flat panel Roman shade

Goblet pleated valance with stationary panels

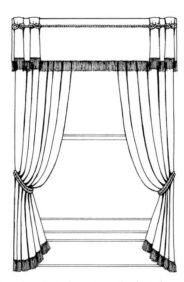

Cartridge pleated cornice with pleated panels

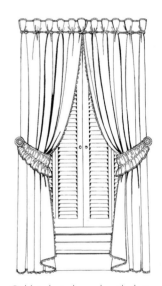

Goblet pleated panels with shutters

Rod pocket valance with traversing panels

Flat rod pocket valance with stationary panels

Box pleated valance, wood cornice and panels

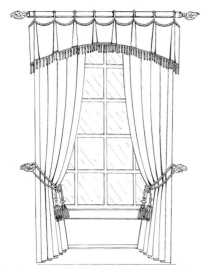

Scalloped ring top valance with inverted pleats,
and tied-back panels

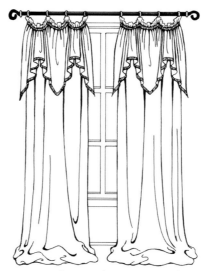

Ring top legacy valances over panels

Wood cornice with puddled
stationary panels

Woood cornice with puddled stationary panels

Upholstered cornice with double panels

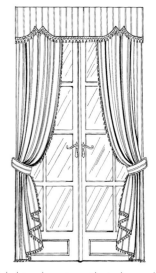

Upholstered cornice with single panels

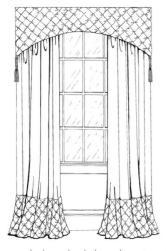

Savannah shaped upholstered cornice with
puddled panels

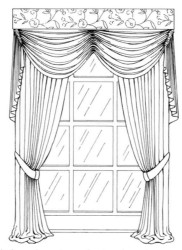

Upholstered cornice with nine-pleated swag and
cascades, puddled panels

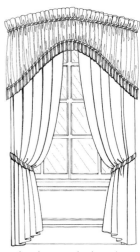

Savannah valance with pleated panels

The Window Decorating Book

Pole swag with drapery panels and flip top bell pulls

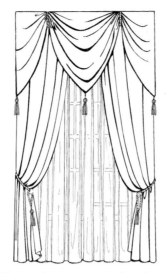

Sheer undertreatment, panels and triangle handkerchief valance

Handkerchief valance with puddled panels

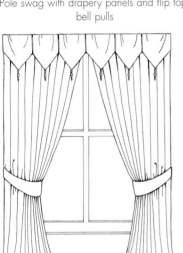

Triangle cornice with puddled panels

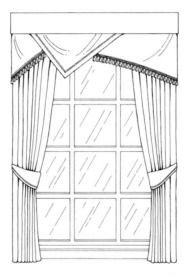

Wood cornice, triangle valance, panels

Triple triangles, panels and wood cornice

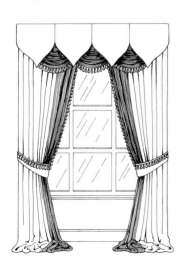

Shirred swags, soft cornice, double panels

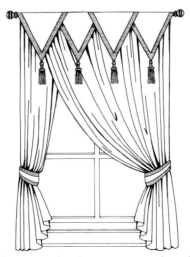

Flip top triangle valance, asymmetrical panels

Upholstered cornice with contrast panels

Appendix 4

Swags & Cascades

Graceful swags and cascades work off the same premise, yet are constructed in various methods to suit your design style. Choose a more rigid box mounted swag for traditional environments; a slouchy pole swag for casual, contemporary designs. Then, as always, add on favoite details to enhance and personalize your treatment.

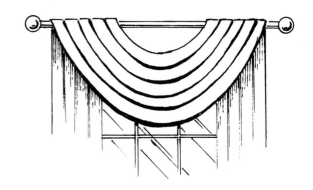

Open swag

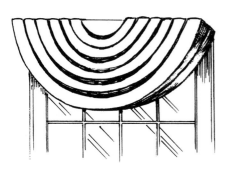

Wrapped swag

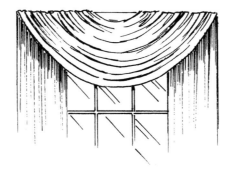

Gathered swag

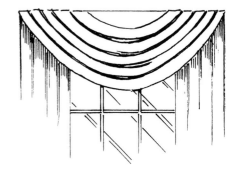

Pleated swag

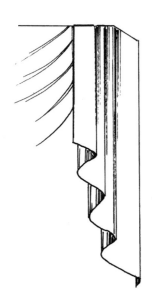

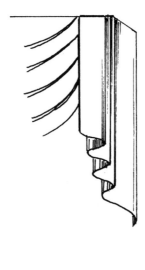

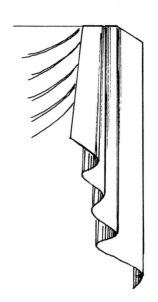

(Left to right): Standard cascade; Stacked cascade; Gathered cascade

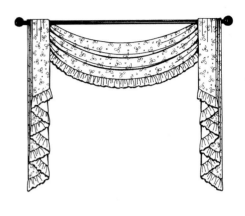

Board-mounted swag and cascade with bow

Ruffled swag and cascade with bow accent

Pole-mounted swag and cascade with ruffle trim

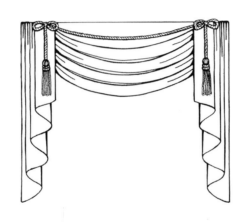

Tailored swag and cascade with button detailing

Board-mounted swag and cascade with tassel and braid detailing

Board-mounted swag, cascades, rosette accent

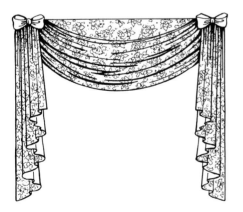

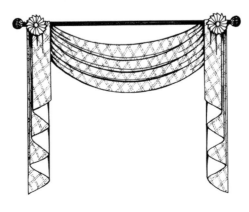

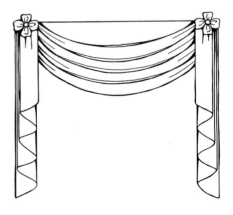

Board-mounted swag, cascade with contrast underlining and bow accents

Pole-mounted swag, cascade, contrast underlinging, rosette accent

Board-mounted swag and jabot with cascades and rosette

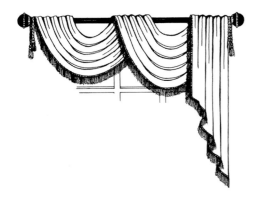

Asymmetrical pole swag with bullion fringe

Symmetrical pole swag

Single swag edged in braid and beads, with rope detailing

Pole mounted swag and cascade with fringe

Classic board-mounted gathered swag and cascade

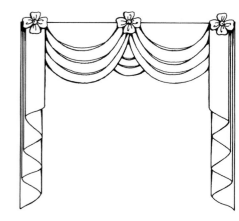

Board-mounted swag with flower accenting

Board-mounted swag and cascade

Board-mounted swag and cascade with jabot and flower accent

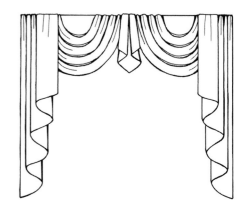

Board-mounted swag, cascade and jabot

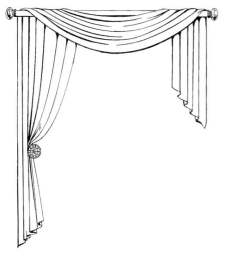

Asymmetrical pole swag

Swag trio with elongated cascades

Pole swag with cascades edged in bullion fringe

Traditional board mounted swag with cascades and jabot

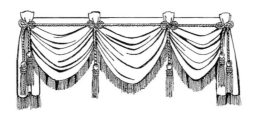

Triple swag, pole mounted with bullion and tassel detailing

Casual overlapping pole swags

Board mounted open swag

Casual pole swag with tied corner detailing

Swags and cascades with jabot and rosette detail

Appendix 5

Draperies & Bed Coverings

As children, we begged for a cozy nest of a bed with fabric roofs. We made play areas out of blankets and card tables, we slept out in tents. There is a coziness and security that a covered bed imparts and luxuriousness that speaks of opulence. Consider bringing the beauty of draperies and other window dressings not just into the bedroom via windows — but also onto the bed itself. Elegance, beauty...these beds have it all.

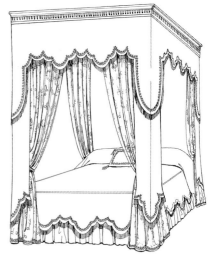

Drapery panels; soft cornice; wood canopy and matching coverlet

Soft cornice; drapery panels; bed skirt and matching bolsters

Swagged panels; scalloped valance; brush fringe and tassel detailing

Box pleated, curved valance;; shirred fabric ceiling; scalloped coverlet; box pleated duster

Upholstered headboard; gathered bedskirt; swag and jabot; drapery panels

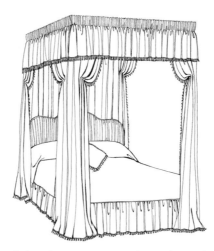

Pencil pleated top treatment; matching side panels; upholstered headboard

Fabric scarves; scalloped coverlet; gathered bedskirt; upholstered headboard

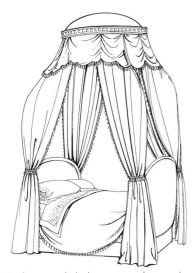

Oval corona; lush drapery panels; coverlet

Crown corona with double Bishop sleeve panels; oversized tassel accents; matching coverlet

Crown corona with cascade and bow accents; upholstered headboard; scalloped gathered bedskirt

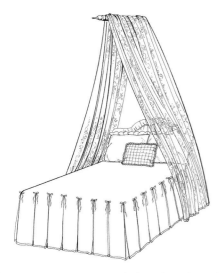

Fabric draped decorative pole; box pleated coverlet

Fabric draped decorative pole secured with large tassel tiebacks; scalloped dust ruffle

Scarf swags with small knotted cascade; upholstered headboard; pleated bedskirt

Box pleated bedskirt; braid-trimmed coverlet; drapery panels; goblet pleated top treatment; back drapery

Wood cornice; fabric valance and drapery panels; dust ruffle; matching coverlet

Arched Kingston valance; draperies; tiebacks; pleated dust ruffle; matching pillows

Half round corona with swag and jabot; swagged coverlet; box pleated dust ruffle

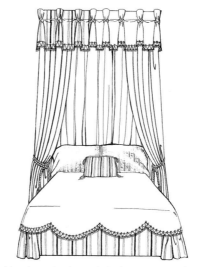

Goblet pleated valance; lush draperies; matching dust ruffle and pillow

Banner-style canopy hung from decorative poles; matching upholstered head and foot board

Scalloped, box pleated valance; pleated drapery panels with scalloped edging; pleated bedskirt

Casual scarf swag hung off angled decorative rods; triangle headboard

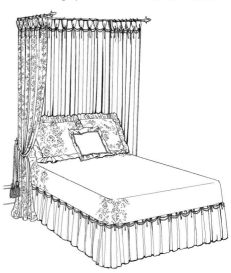

Goblet pleated draperies hung off decorative rods; inverted box pleated dust ruffle

Ruched fabric headboard and corona; pleated drapery panels; matching coverlet

Bishop sleeve panels with swagged cornice; pleated dust ruffle; coordinating pillows

Shell motif cornice; swag and cascade; pleated draperies; matching coverlet; upholstered headboard

Trimmed corona; panels with contrast lining; dust ruffle

Swag-draped corona; pleated draperies; decorative rosettes; pleated dust ruffle; matching coverlet

Soft cornice covered corona; wide drapery panels; ruched, scalloped headboard

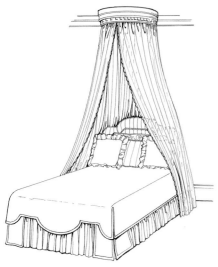

Wood corona; sheer fabric panels; upholstered headboard; scalloped coverlet; box pleated ruffle

Goblet pleated valance; jabots; inverted box pleated dust ruffle; coordinating pillows

Elaborately gathered fabric ceiling with matching duster; drapery panels

Swagged fabric; fabric wall; matching dust ruffle, pillows and headboard

Fabric applied directly to ceiling, then swagged; Austrian-style coverlet

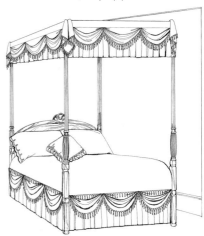

Swags and jabot with tassel trim; box pleated valance and swagged coverlet

Feminine drapery panels; fabric ceiling; bow accents

Masculine box pleating with simple swags and tassel detailing

Sheer drapery panels; pinch pleated dust ruffle; coordinating headboard

Ruched canopy and coverlet; pleated panels

Droopy, inviting swags and jabots; box pleated valance

Tab top panels with matching fabric tie backs; coordinating dust ruffle and pillow

Casually arranged fabric is wrapped organizaclly; coordinating pillows and bedding

Sheer scarf swah arranged asymmetrically; sheer coverlet

Scarf swag with large center jabot couples with lower second swag; coordinating bedskirt

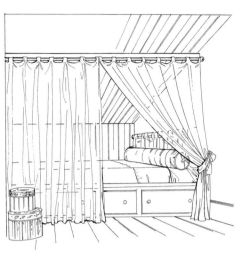

Tab top sheer draperies; tabbed headboard

Soft cornice inset; coorindating coverlet; fabric wall; matching draperies

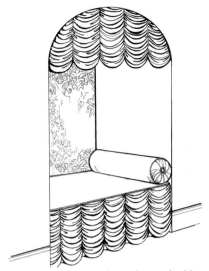

Austrian valance and coordinating bedskirt

Scalloped coverlet; simple floral panels

Tie top panels with simple fabric tiebacks; tie top headboard

Pleated valance and bedskirt with upholstered head-board and drapery panel

Country florals make use of ruffle accenting

Swags with rosette accent; Bishop sleeve panels and upholstered sideboard

Upholstered walls and ceiling; soft cornice with jabot accent; matching bolster

Appendix 6

Hemlines & Headings

We have been looking at plenty of window coverings and now it's time to look at options for the top and bottom of any drapery panel or top treatment. So many wonderful options for personalization.

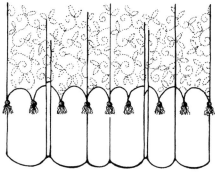
Banding with tassels

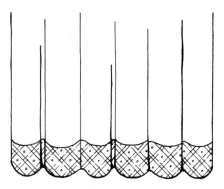
Fabric banding

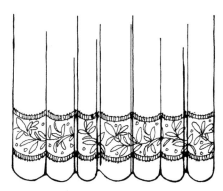
Raised fabric banding

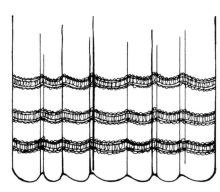
Triple fringe

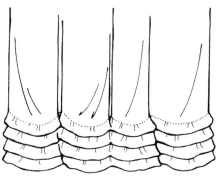
Pleated cuffed hem

Puddled bullion fringe with beads

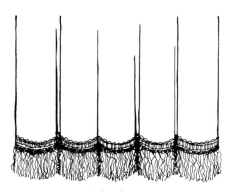
Bullion fringe

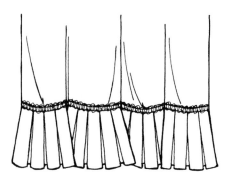
Box pleated hem

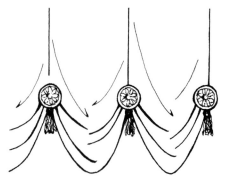
Open hem with rosettes and tassels

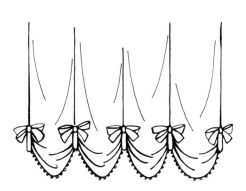
Opera hem with ties

The Window Decorating Book

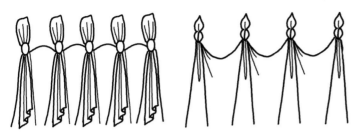

Button accented tabs with extended fabric jabot; Knotted tabs

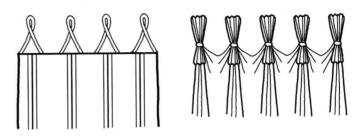

Hourglass gathered tabs; Flat panel drapery with swicthback loops

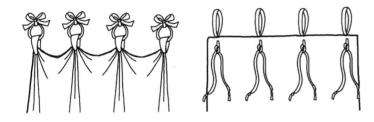

Tab panel with decorative bowshangs on individual hardware pieces; Buttonhole panel with looped skinny tabs

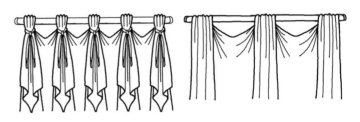

Flip over rod jabot tab header; Waterfall-style gathered tab with swags

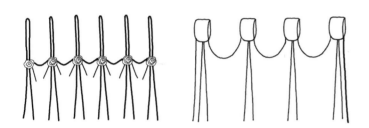

Extended tab loop panel with rosette detailing;Tab top variation

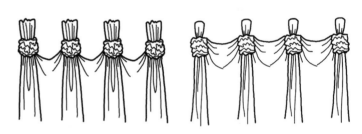

Gathered tabs; Designer ruched tabs with swag detailing on panel

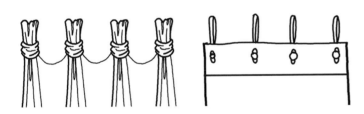

Gathered tabs with contrast fabric sleeves; Looped tab top

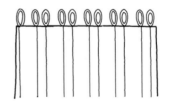

Looped tab top; Tab top variation

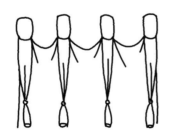

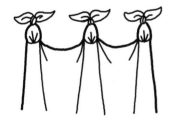

Tied top; Tab top variation

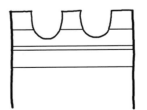

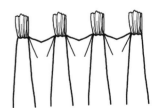

Tab top variation; Triple pleat gathered tabs

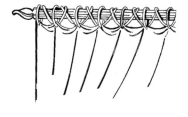
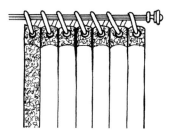
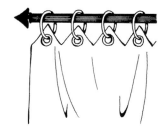

Grommet & tie top; Unusually strung top

String top with grommets; Grommet top with rings

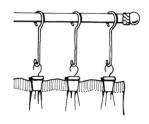
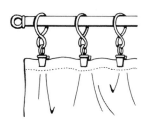
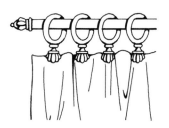
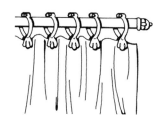

Ring top variations

Ring top variations

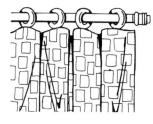
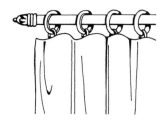
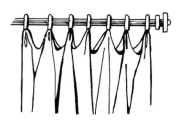

Ring top variation; Clip with ring top

Ring top variations

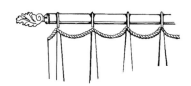

Ring top variations

Ring top variations

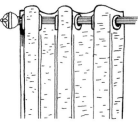
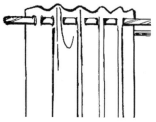
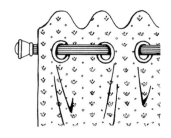
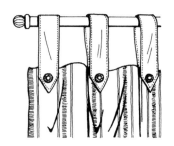

Traditional grommet top variations

Grommet top variation; Tab top

 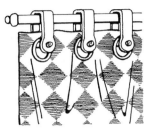

Tab top variations   Tab top variations

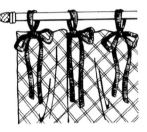 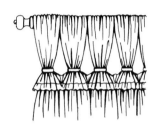

Tie top; Butterfly pleated tab top

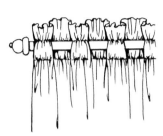 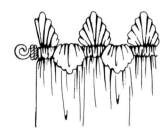

Blouson header with gathered pleats; Shell motif with fabric covered rod &
mock tab top

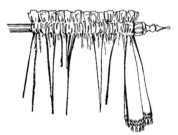 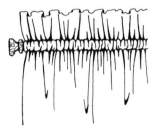

Rod pocket header with ruffle accent top variations

Goblet pleated top; Goblet pleats on arch top window

Stationary medallion hung; Decorative bow over stationary hardware

 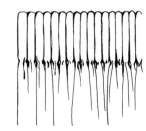

Designer header with lattice work detailing; Pencil pleated rod pocket top

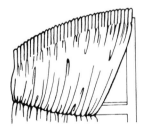 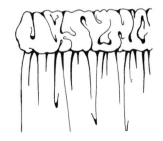

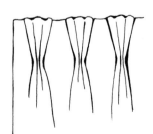 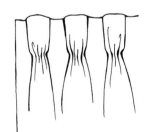

Butterfly pleated drapery hung from sewn in hooks; Slightly gathered cartridge
pleated

Pencil pleated arch top drapery; Blouson top

Folded spiral with choux; daffodil rosette

Petal rosette; accordion fan

Bunched fan; peacock

Choux; shirred spiral

Double choux; knot

Shirred pouf; twisted knot

Pleated rosette; pleated double rosette

Shirred rosette; Maltese cross

Padded Maltese cross; Maltese cross with rosette

Pointed petal rosette; accordion bow

Multi-ribbon bow; ruched square

Ruched doughnut; bow tie

Straight ribbon bow; hanging ribbon bow

Shirred bow; triple petal bow

Bow with rosette accent; thin ribbon bow

Double Maltesel cross; Trefoil

Pointed trefoil; Flame trefoil

Pointed cross; pointed petal cross

Wired ribbon bow; knotted tie

Single pointed tie; double clipped tie

Double angled tie; pointed tie

The Window Decorating Book

Glossary

A

Accordion: A shade with a unique, vertical, folding blade system. Designed to cover a large expanse of glass quickly. *See also* Pleated

Acoustical properties: How a window treatment reacts to various sound waves by absorbing, reflecting or transmitting.

Arch-top: A curtain or drapery for the specialty shaped arch top window. A special frame is constructed with small hooks or pegs to shadow the curved area of the window. Loops are attached to this simple curved top treatment and it is hooked into place. It is a stationary treatment, although the sides can be pulled out of the way.

Austrian: A formal treatment that offers shirred, vertical panels (versus the horizontal panels of the Roman shade). Note that this treatment, when installed and/or created improperly, will have a tendency to pull in on the sides.

B

Bahamas (Bermuda): An exterior shutter, it can be crafted from metal, wood or vinyl. While beautiful, its primary function is security and protection from severe storms. The difference is that this shutter is hinged at the top and opens out from the window like an awning.

Ball fringe: Small balls (such as a pom-pom or even beaded balls) are attached to a flat, raw edge that will be inserted into a seam before it is closed up. A more casual look.

Balloon: A fabric shade made with vertical rows that can be gathered and raised horizontally to the top of the window. Soft and puffy, the treatment is pretty when raised and offers a full, gathered look with inverted pleats. Resembles its cousin, the balloon valance, a stationary treatment.

Baton: A long wand that attaches to the top edge of a drapery. Its main function is to offer an easy way to traverse draperies back and forth without having to touch (and thus, possibly soil) the fabric. Usually, it is hidden in the folds of the draperies when opened and also hangs behind the drapery, rather than in front.

Bishop sleeve: Tieback draperies that have been bloused vertically at least twice and most resemble the puffy sleeve of a fancy garment.

Box pleat: A flat, symmetrical fold of cloth sewn in place to create fullness, spaced evenly across the top of a drapery. The fabric is sometimes folded back on either side of the pleat to show, for example, a contrasting fabric.

Bracket: Typically an indiscrete piece of hardware, the bracket holds the drapery rod in place. Sometimes it is visible, such as at the end of a pole where it is a point of emphasis, but most often, the bracket is a piece of hardware best left hidden.

Braid: Similar to gimp (*see definition*), braid is used primarily to conceal raw edges and seams.

Brocade: Rich and heavy, this multi-colored jacquard (*see definition*) fabric is typically used in upholstery but sometimes in draperies. Occasionally incorporates metallic threads as part of its all-over raised patterns or floral designs. Traditionally created from a background of cotton with rayon/silk patterns.

Brush fringe: A more casual look than bullion, the brush fringe looks very similar to its moniker: like a soft, downy brush. When purchased, the brush fringe will have a long strand of protective chain stitch holding the fringe in place. This thread is only removed after its installation onto the treatment.

Bullion fringe: Long, twisted lengths of rope form a dense fringe. Typically five inches or longer, it is a lush edging for heavier fabric (such as velvet) draperies, although it can be lighter and more casual. It has taken over ruffles as the popular way to edge a treatment.

Burlap: Loosely constructed, this plain-weave jute fabric is most often seen as housing for sacks of coffee beans or as backing on some types of flooring products. However, in recent years, this rough, coarse fabric has made its way into trendy interiors, reinvented as casual draperies.

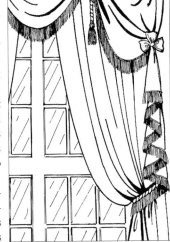

Bullion fringe

Burnout: A technique used on many kinds of fabric but in general is a chemical solution applied to destroy a portion of the fabric, while leaving other areas intact. An example would be burning a floral pattern out of the pile in a velvet piece while leaving the backing fabric intact. Burnout sheers are also extremely popular, as they allow light to filter through at various intensities.

Button: A decorative accent, typically covered with fabric or woven cord, used to provide a small indentation in an upholstered piece such as a cornice or more often, a pillow or arm of an upholstered chair.

C

Café curtain: Designed as a two-tier treatment, café curtains are set at a variety of heights for maximum privacy and light control. They are usually kept closed, though can traverse if necessary.

Café shutter: A smaller-style shutter used to cover only the bottom half of a window, for a combination of privacy and sunshine.

Calico: Used primarily for simple curtains, this cotton fabric boasts small floral patterns (typically) on a contrasting background. An inexpensive fabric, calico is thin and not particularly colorfast, but crisp and pretty when ironed.

Canvas: A sturdy, plain weave cloth, this cotton or cotton/polyester cloth offers a stiff and tailored, yet casual look. Best used for stationary drapery panels. Consider duck or sailcloth (lighter weight canvas) if you require a little bit of draping.

Cascade: A zig-zag shaped piece of fabric falling gracefully from the top of a drapery or top treatment. Can also be called as an ascot or jabot, depending upon the shape and pleat pattern used.

Cellular: *see* Honeycomb

Chintz: This cotton cloth offers bright colors, patterns and floral motifs. Consider having this fabric lined if used in a window that receives direct sunlight. Sometimes chintz is finished with a slight glaze to offer a polished look, although it will wash or wear off with repeated handling. Was very popular in the 18th century, though is still used frequently today due to its lower cost and bright patterns. For curtains or draperies.

Cloud: This fabric shade has a gathered heading that cascades into soft poufs when opened. Similar to the balloon shade, it can be finished with or without a decorative skirt at the bottom edge.

Colorfastness: A material's capacity to resist color change when exposed to sunlight and various liquids.

Cord: Created by twisting or braiding, a cord can be made of a variety of colors and fibers. Typically used as an edging for upholstery but can also be employed on a very heavy drapery panel. Has a "lip" to allow ease of attachment in between seams.

Cornice: A rigid treatment that sometimes serves as a mask for holding attached draperies or for hiding various window treatment hardware or even masking architectural flaws. The cornice is typically constructed of a chip board-style wood or lightweight material over which padding is placed, then covered with a fabric and finished with decorative trim or cording to cover any seams. Only fits across the top of a window frame. A focal point; usually mounted on the outside of a window frame.

Curtain: A simple treatment, typically unlined, usually stationary or possibly hand drawn. Usually hung on a simple rod.

D

Damask: A finer, thinner fabric than brocade, it mixes shiny and dull threads to create beautiful patterns of high luster. Can be crafted of silk, cotton, rayon or linen. Its patterns are usually reversible, an example being two-color damask in which the colors reverse depending upon which side is shown. For draperies.

Dotted Swiss: A pretty, delicate lightweight cotton fabric best suited for curtains. Small raised dots printed on either side of the fabric are the identifying detail. Most often they are woven into the fabric; they can now be found applied to the surface.

Drapery: A heavier treatment, lined, and able to open and close in a number of different ways. Can also be stationary, which typically means it flanks either side of a window, rather than hanging in front of it.

E

Edging: A decorative piece that has one raw edge and one embellished edge.

Embossing: Deliberate texturing (high and low areas) in fabrics (in particular) but also seen in vinyl and faux products. Embossing accomplishes functional and aesthetic goals.

Eyebrow: A sunburst shutter (*see definition*), but it is wider than it is high.

Eyelash fringe: Named because the short, tiny fringe resembles eyelashes. See Fringe (*next page*) for a deeper explanation of this type of passementerie.

F

Fabric/Vane combinations: Fabric/vane combinations are vanes (similar to blind slats) between which fabric has been suspended. Closed, these products look like a regular shade. With the treatment still in a closed position but with the vanes rotated open, they filter the light, thus allowing more control than a regular shade.

Festoon: Folded drapery fabric that hangs in a graceful curve from the top of the window, usually drawn up on cords. Also known as a swag. The term festoon can also refer to a ribbon-tied garland balanced between two points (such as either side of a window), which drapes down in the center.

Finial: A decorative hardware piece attached to the end of a pole or rod, which keeps the drapery from falling off the end.

Fire resistance: The ability of a window treatment to withstand fire or to provide protection from it.

Fire retardant: A chemical used on a window treatment to retard the spread of fire over that surface.

Flip topper: Typically a flat, contrast lined fabric panel that flips over a rod. The flipped portion will frequently be decorated to draw attention, such as using beads or other trim and may also be cinched or triangulated in some way for added emphasis.

Focal point: The major point of interest in a room, such as a fireplace or large window treatment.

French pleat: A three-fold pleat found at the top of a drapery. Also known as a pinch pleat.

Fringe: Available in sizes from about one inch in length to about eighteen inches, fringe is a lighter style of bullion: whereas the bullion is more like twisted rope, fringe is more like multiple threads. Can also be a length of delicate tassels, a row of balls or even beads.

Frog: A two-piece closure made of cord that is wound in a decorative manner. One half of the frog houses the loop; the other houses the knot. Used for decoration.

G

Gimp: A thin, woven braid typically used to cover seams or to mask upholstery tacks or staples. Usually silk or metallic, it is finished on both edges. Can be stitched on or glued.

Gingham: Usually seen in a plaid or checked pattern, gingham is a plain weave cotton fabric used most often for café curtains and very light draperies, such as seen in a child's room. Typically white with one color accent.

Goblet pleat: Similar to a pinch pleat, only the top of the pleat resembles the shape of a goblet. Sometimes the goblet is filled with batting to provide bulk, or a contrasting fabric for emphasis.

Grommet: Used for a modern look on flat paneled draperies, the grommet is installed onto the header of the drapery panel, and then, depending upon the size of the grommet, the rod is slipped through the grommets or the treatment is hung by stringing cording through the grommets for a more unusual look.

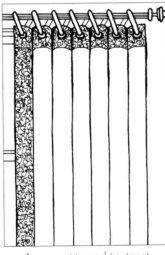

A grommet topped treatment

H

Hand: How a fabric feels when a hand is run over its surface.

Holdback: A piece of hardware placed about one-third to midway between the top and bottom of a window, used to hold draperies back to either side. Typically used in conjunction with a tieback.

Honeycomb: Named after the cellular shape of the comb of the honeybee, honeycomb shades are a flexible, forgiving material that will accomodate any shape window. With the option of single, double or triple honeycombs, these cells trap air, making them perfect for homes requiring sound and thermal insulation. Best, they can be installed either horizontally or vertically, and are available in a variety of material weights, from sheer to complete light blockage. Also known as Cellular shades. Honeycombs are available in a variety of sizes from ⅜" to 2".

Hourglass: A permanently installed treatment that is attached at the top and bottom of, for example, a glass door, and then pinched together in the middle to create the hourglass look. It provides some privacy, but is mostly for decoration.

I

Interfacing: Fabrics used to offer support and give shape to the primary fabric. Some are designed to be stitched to the primary fabric; others can be fused through heat.

Interlining: An insulation of sorts to pad, stiffen and protect the decorative fabric, as well as provide added insulation between the outside and inside of the home. Interlining is sewn to the backside of the beauty fabric and then covered with the lining, which typically faces the street side of the window. Interlining is not seen but provides a great deal of protection and oomph to a drapery panel.

Inverted pleat: Basically, a reverse box pleat, also known as a kick pleat, which conceals the extra fabric in back. The pleat meets in the middle, rather than is folded back at the sides.

Italian stringing: A historical way of drawing fabric in which diagonally strung cords are attached to the back of the drape about one-third of the way down. These cords are manipulated to draw the drapery open and closed. In order for this to work, the top of the drapery must be stationary.

J

Jabot: A decorative stationary side panel used in tandem with a swag (festoon). Also known as a tail.

Jacquard: Refers to a type of weave more so than a fabric. The Jacquard loom was invented in France, 1804 by Joseph Jacquard. Brocade, damask and tapestry are some of the fabrics manufactured with a jacquard attachment, which permits separate control of each of the yarns being processed.

K

Key tassel: A small, decorative tassel (*see definition*) used for accentuating.

Knife pleat: Evenly spaced, tight, crisp, narrow pleats that run vertically across the length of the top of a drapery.

L

Lace: A light, open-work cotton fabric typically used for sheers or curtains, its delicate mesh background consists of openwork designs. On window treatments, it is best to choose a synthetic lace so it will hold its shape when hanging.

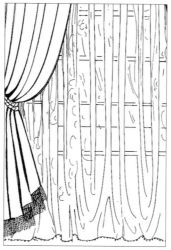
Lace undertreatment

Linen: Stronger and glossier than cotton, linen fibers are obtained from the interior of the woody stem of the flax plant. It is strong but not pliable and will wrinkle readily. However, its tough, textured beauty makes it an interesting look at the window in curtain or drapery form. Excellent sun resistance.

Lining: A layer attached to the backside of a decorative fabric or interlining to protect drapery fabric from sun rays and potential water damage from leaky windows. Adds bulk to a drapery.

Lipcord: A decorative cord to which a narrow piece of fabric (the lip) has been attached. That fabric is slid into an open area (to be seamed) during the construction of a drapery. When the seam is stitched, the cord covers the seamed area, concealing it.

Loop fringe: Similar to brush fringe, only the fringe loops back into the finial or lip cord rather than it being cut at the bottom.

Louvers: Rotating on a pin and connected together by a tilt bar, these individual shutter pieces can vary in size from a typical standard 1¼" inches to over four inches, depending upon the material used and type of shutter product.

M

Matchstick blinds: A shade (not a blind, as the name suggests), similar to woven wood and grass shades. Horizontally-placed sticks of toothpick-thin bamboo are woven together and then will fold up in pleats like a Roman shade or operate like a standard shade. Better used in a sun porch area where the issue of sun filtering is most important.

Matelassé: Meaning "padded" or "quilted" (French), this medium to heavy double cloth fabric is usually made from silk, cotton, rayon or wool. For draperies.

Mesh: Synthetic materials of various densities of weave and color options offer a high-tech look. Typically a roll-up, these shades can be motorized to add to their futuristic appeal.

Moiré: Meaning "watered" (French) this silk, rayon, cotton or acetate fabric has a distinctive wavy pattern on the surface that reflects light in the same way that light reflects off water.

Muslin: For casual curtains and draperies, cotton muslin can be fine to coarsely woven. Typically used as liner fabric, but has been seen as the primary material. Coloration is neutral.

O

Organza (Organdy): This lightweight, crisp, sheer cotton fabric is finished with a starch that will wash out. Will wrinkle quickly if crumpled or not finished with a wrinkle-resistant finish. Can take a variety of finishes and embellishments including bleaching, dying, frosting, flocking and more. For curtains and draperies.

P

Panel: A shutter panel on a track system, or a folding shutter, often used to cover a sliding glass door. Can sometimes have fabric or glass inserts.

Pinch Pleat: *see* French Pleat

Piping: A thin cord covered in fabric that is used primarily to cover seams.

Plaid: Designs consisting of crossed stripes, many of them originating in Scottish tartans.

Plantation shutter: Plantation shutters have louvers over two inches wide and can be over four inches wide. Panels are typically installed into the casement of a window. The larger louver allows for a clearer viewing area when open.

Pleated: A single layer of sturdy fabric with crisp pleats that fold up like an accordion when raised and offer a slight zig-zag look when closed. Fabrics can range from very sheer to totally private and the pleats are usually about one inch in size. Also known as Accordion shades.

Portiere: A drapery treatment that hangs in either a doorway or room entrance. Usually stationary, its main function is to soften and beautify an area. When operational, it can serve as a sound barrier between two rooms and also alleviate drafts.

R

Rails (including top, divider and bottom): These shutter pieces are structural and range in height from approximately two inches to about 4½" inches high depending upon the height of the panel and size of the louver.

Repeat: The distance from the center of one motif of a pattern to the center of the next.

Rick rack: Typically a serpentine-shaped, thin flat braid used for edging, such as on dotted Swiss curtains.

Ring: There are a couple of different uses for the ring, a circular hardware piece available in many different sizes and materials. When more diminuative, it is used in conjunction with a rod and helps the drapery traverse it, sliding from one side to the next. It is also used in conjunction with a drapery hook, which is hidden inside of a pinch pleat at the top of the drapery, for example. When used

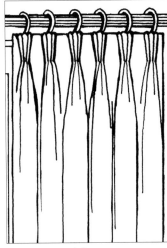

Ring topped drapery treatment

in a larger format, it can become a bracket used to sling a scarf treatment through or offer some type of containment for holding a part of the drapery. Typically, the larger format ring is stationary.

Rod: A straight piece of drapery hardware usually made of wood, polymer or a metal such as wrought iron or steel that is suspended between two points through the use of brackets or rod end holders. Attached at the top of a window frame, or even further up yet at ceiling level, the drapery rod is the foremost piece of hardware used to suspend a window treatment.

Rod pocket: A hollow tube-like sleeve located at the top of a drapery (and sometimes top/bottom of a curtain) that will accommodate a rod. The rod is attached to the wall or ceiling and the drapery, suspending from it, is able to traverse back and forth.

Roller: Vinyl or fabric, this shade is operated with a spring or clutch system that rolls up into a tube when open. Roller shades can be had in anything from sheer to total light blockage, but being a solid piece, can only be so flexible in controlling light. There have been improvements made throughout the years, and the clumsy mechanisms of the past have been replaced with the capability for precise positioning, zero snapback and decorative valances to hide the top of the roller.

Roman: This corded shade has rods set horizontally on the backside of the fabric which, when raised, form a series of sideways pleats, usually about four to six inches deep. The beauty of a Roman shade is that it implies the look and feel of drapery, but it raises and lowers horizontally. Can be made with either flat folds or overlapping folds. Not recommended for window applications wider or longer than 84".

Rosette: A fabric piece used primarily for accentuating. Resembles a flower and can be quite large when used at the top of a drapery, or quite small, such as when used to dot the arm of an upholstered chair. Can also showcase a tassel hanging from the middle.

S

Satin: With a matte back and a lustrous front, satin is available in many colors, weights and degrees of stiffness. Traditionally for evening and wedding garments, as well as high end bedding, it is sometimes at the window. Expensive and slippery but used occasionally for drapery.

Satin finish: A fabric finish with a soft sheen.

Scarf: A single, lengthy piece of lightweight fabric with a color/pattern that shows on both sides (as opposed to simply being imprinted on one side) that either wraps loosely around a stationary rod, or loops through decorative brackets placed on either side of a window frame.

Shade: A color produced by adding black to a pigment. Can also be a change in an appearance of a fabric (such as velvet) due to the slant or tilt of fibers — a reflection of light.

Sheer: A light, typically see-through or opaque fabric, never lined. It is only used for beauty and some sun control. Usually used in conjunction with some other hard treatment, such as cellular shades or blinds.

Shirred: A traditional Roman shade taken one step further to offer romantic shirring on each of the pleats. An elegant look. For best effect, soft, drapeable fabrics are suggested.

Shutter blinds: Combines the larger louvers of the shutter with the ease of blind operation. Resemble wood blinds.

Silk: One of the first materials used for draperies, silk is a natural filament, a product the silk worm creates when constructing its cocoon. There are many kinds of silk: tussah (a wild silk which is shorter and wider), shantung (raw and irregular) and doupioni (uneven and irregular threads) to name a few. Shiny and luxurious, it is a beautiful choice for drapery panels but will be affected by sun and water. It is best to line and interline this fabric when used at the window, to protect it and lengthen its life.

Solar shade: A spectacular tool to control the harmful rays of the sun, solar shades filter and diffuse bright sunlight without sacrificing the view. A downside is that most solar shades are not meant to offer privacy, so they are best used in conjunction with another treatment, such as a drapery.

Stain resistant: The degree to which a window treatment can resist permanent discoloration and soiling.

Stationary drape: Usually hangs to either side of the window and acts as decoration. It is not meant to provide protection from the sun or offer privacy. It is a beauty treatment that does not move.

Stiles: The right and left structural pieces, which aid in holding the shutter together. Usually about two inches wide and holds the pins in place that connect to the louver.

Sunburst: Typically constructed in the shape of an arch, the sunburst pattern is so named due to its design in the form of "rays" all emanating from a central point usually on the bottom edge of the piece.

Swag & Tail: A section of draped fabric at the top of the window that resembles a sideways "C" shape (swag) coupled with a vertical "tail" which hangs on either side of the swag. Usually has at least three folds although can be up to seven.

T

Tab/tie: A series of tabs at the top of the drapery, either a closed loop or a tie, which a rod either slides through, or the treatment is tied to.

Taffeta: A crisp fabric known best for its wonderful "rustle" sound, taffeta is a lustrous plain weave fabric usually made from synthetic fibers but sometimes made from silk. Best used for draperies, it has a crisp hand and a lot of bulk.

Tapestry: Heavy and deliciously dense, tapestry is often hand-woven and features elaborate motifs such as pictorials, floral and historical scenes. While it is never used for curtains, tapestries are frequently used as wall hangings and occasionally fitted with rod pockets to hang in front of a window.

Tie top drapery header

Tassel: Consisting of three main parts: the cord (used to suspend the tassel), the top (holds the fringe in place, can also be called a finial) and the skirt (the fringe that hangs from inside the top of the piece), a tassel can range from very simple (such as a key tassel) to extremely heavy and ornate. Can either have a "cut" skirt (the yarn is trimmed at the bottom) or a looped skirt, in which the yarn loops down from the finial and then back up inside.

Tassel tieback

Tent fold: A drapery that is constructed so as to resemble an old fashioned pup tent opening, in that the middle edge of the treatment is pulled back and secured simply, overlapping the rest of the drapery, rather than pulling it back as well. Will conceal much of the window, even when open.

Tieback: A shaped piece of fabric or cording used to pull a drapery panel away from a window.

Tilt bar: Connected to each of the individual louvers in the center, the tilt bar controls the light, privacy and ventilation associated with the shutter. Usually moves only up and down.

Tint: A color produced when a pigment is mixed with white.

Toile: French for fabric or cloth, toile is best known as *Toile de Jouy*, a finely printed design resembling a pen and ink drawing. Found primarily on cotton fabric, toile de jouy depicts romantic, idyllic scenes of pastoral countrysides, florals and historical motifs. For curtains and draperies.

Tone-on-tone: A pattern using two or more variations of the same hue to create depth and interest.

V

Valance: A simple to elaborate treatment, the valance is a piece of decorative fabric usually hung from a rod, a piece of decorative hardware or a board. Valances can take on many shapes: poufed, scalloped, pointed, arched, and rectangular and can also be pleated or gathered.

Velvet: Plain and figured velvets are beautiful and soft, and best employed as drapery fabric. A medium weight cut-pile fabric typically constructed of silk, rayon, cotton or synthetics, its high luster and smooth hand create beautiful, graceful folds of fabric. Crease resistant and fairly inexpensive, velvet wears well and should be cut simply to accentuate its clean lines.

Voile: A lightweight, sheer fabric, cotton (also wool) voile is plain and loosely woven. Perfect for curtains or draperies, it gathers and drapes well.

W

Wood: This natural product offers both beauty and strength. Its grain is unmatched in appearance; no two pieces could ever be absolutely alike. Used for cornices and decorative hardware. As always, wood is recyclable.

Wool: A natural animal fiber that captures dye well, and is soft and versatile.

Woven grass/wood: Beautiful blends of wood, bamboo, reeds and grasses make woven shades a natural, warm choice, but they require more stacking space than the thinner honeycomb and pleated shades. Banding options add a beautiful finishing touch. Request a privacy backing if you want them to do more than filter light. *See also* Matchstick blinds.

Index

Resources

Books

Bugg, Carol Donayre, *Smart & Simple Decorating*, TIME-LIFE BOOKS, Alexandria, VA, 1999

Coleman, Brian D., *Scalamandré: Luxurious Home Interiors*, Gibbs Smith, Salt Lake City, UT, 2004

Demir, M., *Home Fashions Fourth Edition*, Charles Randall, Inc., Orange, CA, 2005

Evelegh, Tessa, *House Beautiful Window Workshop*, Hearst Books, a division of Sterling Publishing Co., Inc., NY, NY, 2004

Gibbs, Jenny, *Curtains and Draperies: History, Design, Inspiration*, The Overlook Press, Woodstock, NY, 1994

Home, Traditional, *Traditional Home® Window Style*, Meredith Corporation, Des Moines, IA, 2002

Homeowner, Creative, *The New Smart Approach to Home Decorating*, Creative Homeowner® A Division of Federal Marketing Corp., Upper Saddle River, NJ, 2003

Hoppen, Stephanie, *The New Curtain Book*, A Bulfinch Press Book, Boston • New York • London, 2003

Jones, Chester, *Colefax and Fowler The Best in English Interior Decoration*, A Bulfinch Press Book, Boston • New York • Toronto • London, 1989

Linton, Mary Fox, *Window Style*, A Bulfinch Press Book, Boston • New York • London, 2000

Miller, Judith, *Influential Styles*, Watson-Guptill Publications, New York, NY, 2003

Miller, Judith, *Judith Miller's Guide to Period-Style Curtains and Soft Furnishings*, The Overlook Press, Woodstock, NY, 1996

Parks, Carol, *Complete Book of Window Treatments & Curtains*, Sterling Publishing Co., Inc., New York, NY, 1995

Randall, Charles T., *The Encyclopedia of Window Fashions Sixth Edition*, Charles Randall, Inc., Orange, CA, 2006

Whitemore, Maureen, *Home Furnishings Workbook*, Charles Randall, Inc., Orange, CA, 1999

Source Guide

The authors wish to thank the following companies and individuals for help in providing information and photography for The *Window Decorating Book*.

Opening pages 1–15

>Cover: Casa Fiora, casafiora.com, photo courtesy of Casa Fiora; Inside front: Hunter Douglas Window Fashions, hunterdouglas.com

>Title page: Jamie Gibbs & Associates,.jamiegibbsassociates.com, photo by Bill Geddes; Copyright page & Contents: Houles et Cie, houles.com

>6–7: Interiors by Decorating Den, decoratingden.com, 800.dec.dens

>8–9: Stroheim & Romann, stroheim.com

>10: Interiors by Decorating Den, decoratingden.com

>11: Paris Texas Hardware, paristexashardware.com

>12: Springs Window Fashions/Graber, springs.com

>13: Hunter Douglas Window Fashions, hunterdouglas.com

>14–15: Photos courtesy of DreamDraper

Shutters Chapter

>16–17: Hunter Douglas Window Fashions, hunterdouglas.com

>18: Comfortex Window Fashions, comfortex.com

>19: Aveno Window Fashions, aveno.com, photograph courtesy of Aveno, Inc.

>20: Smith+Noble, smithandnoble.com

>21: (top & bottom) Hunter Douglas Window Fashions, hunterdouglas.com

>22: Casa Fiora, casafiora.com, photo courtesy of Casa Fiora

>23: Springs Window Fashions/Graber, springs.com

>24: Aveno Window Fashions, aveno.com, photograph courtesy of Aveno, Inc.

>25: Hunter Douglas Window Fashions, hunterdouglas.com

>26: SMI-Kirtz Shutters, kirtz.com

>27: SMI-Kirtz Shutters, kirtz.com

>28: Smith+Noble, smithandnoble.com

>29: SMI-Kirtz Shutters, kirtz.com

>30: Lafayette Interior Fashions, lafvb.com;

>31: Smith+Noble, smithandnoble.com

>32: (top) SMI-Kirtz Shutters, kirtz.com; (bottom) Springs Window Fashions/ Graber, springs.com;

>33: Mary Ann Angara-Romano, INTERIORS by ROMANO, interiorsbyromano.com

>34: (top) Comfortex Window Fashions, comfortex.com; (left) SMI-Kirtz Shutters, kirtz.com; (right) ITA Inc., itainc.net

>35: Houston Shutters, houstonshutters.com

>36: (left) Hunter Douglas Window Fashions, hunterdouglas.com; (right) Houston Shutters, houstonshutters.com

>38–39: Interiors by Decorating Den, decoratingden.com, 800.dec.dens

>40 (top): Interiors by Decorating Den, decoratingden.com, 800.dec.dens; (lower left & right) Sarah Barnard, Sarah Barnard Design, sarahbarnard.com

>41: Interiors by Decorating Den, decoratingden.com, 800.dec.dens

>42: Interiors by Decorating Den, decoratingden.com, 800dec.dens

>43: Withers Industries, withersind.com; Interiors by Decorating Den, decoratingden.com, 800dec.dens

>44–45: Shutterstock; shutterstock.com

>46–47: Smith+Noble, smithandnoble.com

Curtains & Draperies Chapter

>48: Photo courtesy of David Duncan Livingston, davidduncanlivingston.com

>49: Donna Elle, Interiors by Donna Elle, donnaelle.com, photograph courtesy of Jeff Allen

>50: Interiors by Decorating Den, decorating den.com, 800.dec.dens;

>51: Interiors by Decorating Den, decoratingden .com, 800.dec.dens

>52: Donna Elle, donnaelle.com, photo courtesy of Jeff Allen

>53: Castec, Inc., castec.com

>54–55: Emily B. Walser, ASID, From Start to Finish Interiors, fstfinteriors.com, photograph courtesy of Dustin Peck, Dustin Peck Photography

>56: Sandy Powell, Signature Draperies & Design, sandypowell@mindspring.com, photograph by Michael Paiva

>57: Carlette Cormier, CC's Designs, ccsdes@comcast.net, photograph by Richard Leo Johnson

>58–59: Casa Fiora, casafiora.com, photo courtesy of Casa Fiora

>60–61: ADO USA, ado-usa.com

>62: (top left) ADO USA, ado-usa.com; (top middle) Donna Elle, Interiors by Donna Elle, donnaelle.com; (top right) Smith+Noble, smithandnoble.com; (bottom left) Smith+Noble, smithandnoble.com; (bottom middle) Digital Vision; (bottom right) Smith+Noble, smithandnoble.com

>63: (top left) Linda Yackle, My Window Designs, teepro3@sbcglobal.net; (top middle) Jeanelle Dech, Crab Apple Farm Interiors, crabapplefarm.com; (top right) ADO USA, ado-usa.com; (middle left) Castec, Inc., castec.com; (middle) Smith+Noble, smithand noble.com; (middle right) Jeanelle

Dech, Crab Apple Farm Interiors, crabapplefarm.com; (bottom left) Castec, Inc., castec.com; (bottom middle) Donna Elle, Interiors by Donna Elle, donnaelle.com, photograph by Jeff Allen; (bottom right) Conso® Products Company, conso.com

>64: Smith+Noble, smithandnoble.com

>65: (left) Emily B. Walser, ASID, From Start to Finish Interiors, fstfinteriors.com, photograph courtesy of Dustin Peck, Dustin Peck Photography; (right) Smith+Noble, smithandnoble.com

>66–67: Shutterstock, shutterstock.com

>68: Casa Fiora, casafiora.com, photo courtesy of Casa Fiora

>69: Stroheim & Romann, stroheim.com;

>70: Smith+Noble, smithandnoble.com

>71: Shutterstock; shutterstock.com

>72: (left) Stroheim & Romann, stroheim.com; (middle) M. Demir, homefashion.com

>73: Calico Corners, calicocorners.com

>74–75: ADO USA, ado-usa.com

>76: (top) Interiors by Decorating Den, decoratingden.com, 800.dec.dens; (bottom) Smith+Noble, smithandnoble.com

>77: Casa Fiora, casafiora .com, photo courtesy of Casa Fiora

>78: (left) Stroheim & Romann, stroheim.com; (right) Sarah Barnard, Sarah Barnard Design, sarahbarnard.com, photograph by Scott Van Dyke; (lower left) Interiors by Decorating Den, decoratingden.com, 800.dec.dens

>79: Interiors by Decorating Den, decoratingden .com, 800.dec.dens

>80: S. A. Maxwell Co., samaxwell.com

>81: (above) Houles et Cie, houles.com; (below) Interiors by Decorating Den, decoratingden.com, 800.dec.dens

>82: (top) Donna Elle, Interiors by Donna Elle, donnaelle.com, photography by Jeff Allen; (bottom) Castec, Inc., castec.com

>83: (top) S. A. Maxwell Co., samaxwell.com; (bottom) Smith+Noble, smithandnoble.com

>84: (left) Smith+Noble, smithandnoble.com; (right) Interiors by Decorating Den, decoratingden.com, 800.dec.dens

>85: Photograph courtesy of David Duncan Livingston, davidduncanlivingston.com

>86: (top left) Interiors by Decorating Den, decoratingden.com, 800.dec.dens; (middle left) Interiors by Decorating Den, decoratingden.com, 800.dec.dens; (lower left) Casa Fiora, casafiora.com, photo courtesy of Casa Fiora; (right) Interiors by Decorating Den, decoratingden.com, 800.dec.dens

>87: Jamie Gibbs & Associates, jamiegibbsassociates.com

>88 (both) Shutterstock, shutterstock.com

>89: (left) Shutterstock, shutterstock.com; (right) Interiors by Decorating Den, decoratingden.com, 800.dec.dens

>90–91: Shutterstock, shutterstock.com

>92: Shutterstock, shutterstock.com; Armstrong World Industries, armstrong.com

>93–94: Shutterstock, shutterstock.com

>95: Sarah Barnard, Sarah Barnard Design, sarahbarnard.com

>96–97: Interiors by Decorating Den, decoratingden.com, 800.dec.dens

>98: Shutterstock, shutterstock.com

>103: Sarah Barnard, Sarah Barnard Design, sarahbarnard.com

>103: ADO USA, ado-usa.com

>104–105: Seabrook Wallcoverings, seabrook.com

>106: Smith+Noble, smithandnoble.com

>107: Conso® Products Company, conso.com

>108–109: Seabrook Wallcoverings, seabrook.com

Blinds Chapter

>110–111: Smith+Noble, smithandnoble.com

>112: Legacy Window Coverings, retroblinds.com

>113: Hunter Douglas Window Fashions, hunterdouglas.com

>114: Smith+Noble, smithandnoble.com

>115: (top) Comfortex Window Fashions, comfortex.com; (bottom) Interiors by Decorating Den, decoratingden.com, 800.dec.dens

>116: Interiors by Decorating Den, decoratingden.com, 800.dec.dens;

>117: (top) Smith+Noble, smithandnoble.com; (bottom) Comfortex, comfortex.com;

>118: Aveno Window Fashions, aveno.com, photograph courtesy of Aveno, Inc.

>119: Legacy Blinds, Legacy Window Coverings, retroblinds.com

>120: Springs Window Fashions/Graber, springs.com

>121: Hunter Douglas Window Fashions, hunterdouglas.com

>122: Hunter Douglas Window Fashions, hunterdouglas.com

>123: Aveno Window Fashions, aveno.com, photograph courtesy of Aveno, Inc.

>124–125: Smith+Noble, smithandnoble.com

>126: (left) Aveno Window Fashions, aveno.com, photograph courtesy of Aveno, Inc.; (middle) Hunter Douglas Window Fashions, hunterdouglas.com

>127: Smith+Noble, smithandnoble.com

>128: (top) Interiors by Decorating Den, decoratingden.com, 800.dec.dens (lower left) Hunter Douglas Window Fashions, hunterdouglas .com; (lower right) Sherwin Williams, sherwinwilliams.com

>129: Interiors by Decorating Den, decoratingden .com, 800.dec.dens

>130–131: Shutterstock, shutterstock.com

Shades Chapter

>132–133: Calico Corners, calicocorners.com

Combinations Chapter

randall.com

>189: S. A. Maxwell Co.,
samaxwell.com

>190 Smith+Noble,
smithandnoble.com

>191: (left) Emily B. Walser, ASID,
From Start to Finish Interiors,
fstfinteriors.com, photograph courtesy of Dustin Peck, Dustin Peck
Photography; (right) ADO USA,
ado-usa.com

Top Treatments Chapter

>192–193: Interiors by Decorating
Den, decoratingden.com,
800.dec.dens

>194: Interiors by Decorating Den,
decoratingden.com, 800.dec.dens

>195: Smith+Noble, smithandno-
ble.com

>196: Eeta Sachon, Interiors by Eeta,
interiorsbyeeta.com, photograph by
Bill Fish

>197 (top) Interiors by Decorating
Den, decoratingden.com,
800.dec.dens;
(bottom) Interiors by Decorating
Den, decoratingden.com,
800.dec.dens

>198: Interiors by Decorating Den,
decoratingden.com, 800.dec.dens

>199: Calico Corners,
calicocorners.com

>200–201: Interiors by Decorating
Den, decoratingden.com,
800.dec.dens

>202: Design by Kari Kahal,
Creative Designing, Photograph
courtesy of Charles T. Randall, ran-
dallonline.com

>203 (top) Judy Wilfong, Windows
& Walls, windows-and-walls.com,
photograph by Lauri Bridgeforth;
(bottom) Interiors by Decorating
Den, decoratingden.com,
800.dec.dens

>204: (top left) Dahli de-Leon Brant,
CCIDC, ASID, Capital Designs
West, dahlicdw@aol.com; (top mid-
dle) Smith+Noble, smithand
noble.com; (top right)
Smith+Noble, smithandnoble.com;
(lower left) Remember When©
Waverly. Reprinted with permission.
All rights reserved, waverly.com;
(lower middle) Donna Terry,

Interiors by…Donna Terry,
donnaterry1@comcast.net, photograph by Peter Jaquith; (lower right)
Rainbow Woods Inc., rainbow-
woods.com, photograph by Rod
Robinson

>205: (top left) Karen Bunch, Karen
Bunch Designs, karenbunchde-
signs@comcast.net; (top middle)
Sandy Powell, Signature Draperies
& Design, sandypowell@mind-
spring.com, photograph by Michael
Paiva; (top right) Conso® Products
Company, conso. com; (middle left)
Linda Tully, Custom Coverings,
photograph by Donna Jane
Photography; (middle) M. Demir,
homefashion.com; (middle right)
Smith+Noble, smithandnoble.com;
(lower left) Design by Kari Kahal,
Creative Designing, Photograph
courtesy of Charles T. Randall, ran-
dallonline. com; (lower middle) M.
Demir, homefashion.com; (lower
right) ADO USA, ado-usa.com;

>206: (top) Castec, Inc., castec.com;
(bottom) Rainbow Woods Inc.,
rainbowwoods.com

>207: Emily B. Walser, ASID, From
Start to Finish Interiors,
fstfinteriors.com, photograph courtesy of Dustin Peck, Dustin Peck
Photography

>208: (left) Calico Corners, calico-
corners.com; (middle)
Smith+Noble, smithandnoble.com;

>209: Castec, Inc., castec.com;

>210: (top) Margarett DeGange,
M.Ed, DeGangi Interiors, decorat-
ingschool.com; (bottom) Teresa
Grysikiewicz, Interior Attire,
curtainpro@aol.com

>211: (top) ADO USA, ado-
usa.com; (bottom) Kenny Greene,
Greene Designs, greenedesigns.net

>212: (above) Beth Hodges, Beth
Hodges' Soft Furnishings, bhodges-
dec@aol.com, window design by
Pam DeCuir, photograph by Rob
Garbarini; (below-both)
Smith+Noble, smithandnoble.com

>213: Elaine Addison, Addison
Interiors, addisononteriors.com,
photograph by Greg Page;

>214: (top) Marcye Philbrook,
Marcye Philbrook Design Studio,
marcye.philbrook@verizon.net,
photograph by Marcye Philbrook;

(bottom) Kenny Greene, Greene
Designs, greenedesigns.net

>215: (top) Kathie Chrisicos,
Chrisicos Interior Design, chrisi-
cos.com; (bottom) Smith+Noble,
smithandnoble.com

>216: (left) Interiors by Decorating
Den, decoratingden.com,
800.dec.dens; (right) Interiors by
Decorating Den,
decoratingden.com, 800.dec.dens

>217: (left) Interiors by Decorating
Den, decoratingden.com,
800.dec.dens; (right) Jamie Gibbs &
Associates,
jamiegibbsassociates.com

>218: (left) Carlette Cormier, CC's
Designs, ccsdes@comcast.net, photograph by Richard Leo Johnson;
(middle) Smith+Noble, smithand-
noble.com

>219: Carlette Cormier, CC's
Designs, ccsdes@comcast .net,
photograph by Richard Leo
Johnson

>220: (left) Interiors by Decorating
Den, decoratingden.com,
800.dec.dens; (middle) Shutterstock,
shutterstock.com

>221: Shutterstock. shutterstock.com

>222–223: Interiors by Decorating
Den, decoratingden.com,
800.dec.dens

>224–225: Interiors by Decorating
Den, decoratingden.com,
800.dec.dens

>226: (top) Interiors by Decorating
Den, decoratingden.com,
800.dec.dens; (bottom) Photo courtesy of Pensacola Symphony
Showhouse 2007, pcolasympho-
nyshowhouse.com

>227: (top) Interiors by Decorating
Den, decoratingden.com,
800.dec.dens;
(bottom) Shutterstock, shutter-
stock.com

>228: Interiors by Decorating Den,
decoratingden.com, 800.dec.dens

>230: Rainbow Woods, Inc.,
rainbowwoods.com

>231: Conso® Products Company,
conso.com

>232: Photo courtesy of Charles
Randall, Inc.

>233: Interiors by Decorating Den,
decoratingden.com, 800.dec.dens

>234–235: both Interiors by

Decorating Den, decoratingden.com, 800.dec.dens
>236: Smith+Noble, smithandnoble.com;
>237: Interiors by Decorating Den, decoratingden.com, 800.dec.dens
>238: Interiors by Decorating Den, decoratingden.com, 800.dec.dens
>239: Shutterstock, shutterstock.com
>240–241: Interiors by Decorating Den, decoratingden.com, 800.dec.dens

Dec. Hdwr & Trims Chapter

>242–243: Smith+Noble, smithandnoble.com
>244: Brimar®, brimarinc.com;
>245: Interiors by Decorating Den, decoratingden.com, 800.dec.dens
>246: Houles et Cie, houles .com
>247: (top) Interiors by Decorating Den, decoratingden.com, 800.dec.dens; (bottom) Margarett DeGange, M.Ed, DeGangi Interiors, decoratingschool.com
>248: Houles et Cie, houles.com
>249: Donna Elle, Donna Elle Interior Design, donnaelle.com; photograph by Jeff Allen
>250: Stroheim & Romann, stroheim, com; 251: Houles et Cie, houles.com
>252: Jamie Gibbs & Associates, jamiegibbsassociates.com
>253: Conso® Products Company, conso.com
>254: (top left) Conso® Products Company, conso .com; (top middle) K-Blair Finials, k-blairfinials.com; (top right, middle left) Smith+Noble, smithandnoble.com; (middle) K-Blair Finials, k-blairfinials.com; (middle right) Smith+Noble, smithandnoble.com (lower right) Brimar®, brimarinc.com
>255: (top left) Brimar®, brimarinc.com; (top middle) Conso® Products Company, conso.com; (top right) Suzanne Blackwelder, Sew It Seams, 318.927.2997, photograph by Jeff Scott; (middle left) Donna Elle, Donna Elle Interior Design, donnaelle.com, photograph by Jeff

Allen; (middle) Brimar®, brimarinc.com; (middle right) ADO USA; ado-usa.com; (lower left) Conso® Products Company, conso.com; (lower middle) Smith+Noble, smithandnoble.com; (lower right) Houles et Cie, houles.com;
>256: Smith+Noble, smithandnoble.com
>257: K-Blair Finials, k-blairfinials.com
>258: (left) Houles et Cie, houles.com; (middle) Stroheim & Romann/JAB Decorative Hardware, stroheim.com;
>259: (Above) Smith+Noble, smithandnoble.com; Judy Wilfong, Windows & Walls, windows-and-walls.com, photograph by Lauri Bridgeforth
>260: (top) Margarett DeGange, M.Ed, DeGangi Interiors, decoratingschool.com; (lower left) Paris Texas Hardware, paristexashardware.com; (lower right) K-Blair Finials, k-blairfinials.com
>261: Springs Window Fashions/Graber, springs. com
>262: Conso® Products Company, conso.com
>263: (left) Bomar Trimming, bomartrim.com; (right) Brimar®, brimarinc.com
>264: Interiors by Decorating Den, decoratingden.com, 800.dec.dens
>265: (left column) Paris Texas Hardware, paristexashardware.com; (right) Interiors by Decorating Den, decoratingden.com, 800.dec.dens
>266 (top) Casa Fiora, casafiora.com, photo courtesy of Casa Fiora; (bottom) Conso® Products Company, conso .com
>267: (top) Interiors by Decorating Den, decoratingden.com, 800.dec.dens; (bottom) Elaine Addison, Addison Interiors, addisononteriors.com, photograph by Greg Page
>268: (left) Smith+Noble, smithandnoble.com; (right) S. A. Maxwell Co., samaxwell.com
>269: M. Demir, homefashion.com
>270: Shutterstock, shutterstock.com
>271: (top left) Shutterstock, shutterstock.com; (middle left) Interiors by Decorating Den, decoratingden.com, 800.dec.dens;

(bottom left) Shutterstock, shutterstock.com; (right) Shutterstock, shutterstock.com
>272: (left) Interiors by Decorating Den, decoratingden.com, 800.dec.dens; (middle) Shutterstock, shutterstock.com
>273: Interiors by Decorating Den, decoratingden.com, 800.dec.dens
>274–278: Shutterstock, shutterstock.com
>279: ADO USA, ado-usa.com

Alternatives Chapter

>280: Aveno Window Fashions, aveno.com, photograph courtesy of Aveno, Inc.
>281: Aveno Window Fashions, aveno.com, photograph courtesy of Aveno, Inc.
>282: Springs Window Fashions/Graber, springs.com;
>283: Design Shoji, designshoji.com, photograph by Brian Consterdine
>284: Smith+Noble, smithandnoble.com
>285: (top) Indian Creek Design Studios, indiancreekleather.com; (bottom) Sandy Powell, Signature Draperies & Design, sandypowell@mindspring.com, photograph by Michael Paiva
>286: Rainbow Woods Inc., rainbowwoods.com
>287: Shutterstock, shutterstock.com

Miscellaneous End Pages

>323, 329, 331, 332: Paris Texas Hardware, paristexashardware.com;
>Back cover: Shutterstock, shutterstock.com